THE INDIAN PEAKS WILDERNESS AREA
A HIKING AND FIELD GUIDE

John A. Murray / Foreword by Tim Wirth

PRUETT PUBLISHING COMPANY
Boulder, Colorado

Copyright 1985 by John A. Murray
All rights reserved.

First Edition
1 2 3 4 5 6 7 8 9

Library of Congress Cataloging in Publication Data

Murray, John A., 1954-
   The Indian Peaks Wilderness Area.

    Bibliography: p.
    Includes index.
    1. Hiking—Colorado—Indian Peaks Wilderness—
Guide-books. 2. Indian Peaks Wilderness (Colo.)—
Guide-books. I. Title.
GV199.42.C62I536   1985   917.88'53   85-3631
ISBN 0-87108-690-5 (pbk.)

Printed in the United States of America

ISBN: 0-87108-690-5

Contents

Foreword by U.S. Senator Tim Wirth ix
Epigraph by Theodore Roosevelt xi
Acknowledgements xiii
Preface xv

PART I: NATURAL HISTORY 1
  Archaeology and Human History 2
  Fauna and Flora 6
  Geomorphology and Geography 14
  Climatology 17
  The Upper Montane Forest 19
  The Subalpine Forest 20
  The Alpine Tundra 23

PART II: BACK COUNTRY TRAVEL 28
  Weather 29
  A Wilderness Ethic 33
  A Note on Technical Climbing 34
  Cameras in the High Country 35
  Equipment in Primitive Areas 36
  Important Addresses and Information 39
  New Rules and Regulations 41
  Hazards in the Wilderness 42
  Hunting and Fishing 49

PART III: WILDERNESS TRAILS 50
  Trails West of the Divide 51
  Arapaho Pass Trail 53
  Caribou Pass Trail 59
  Corona Trail 63
  High Lonesome Trail 67
  Cascade Creek Trail 70

    Crater Lake Trail 76
    Hell Canyon Trail 80
    Buchanan Pass Trail 84
    Gourd Lake Trail 88
    Roaring Fork Trail 92
    Knight Ridge Trail 96

Trails East of the Divide 98
    Pawnee Pass Trail 100
    Mitchell Lake Trail 107
    Beaver Creek Trail 110
    Mount Audubon Trail 113
    Arapaho Glacier Trail 118
    Arapaho Pass Trail 120
    King Lake Trail 124
    Devil's Thumb Lake Trail 128
    St. Vrain Mountain Trail................... 132
    St. Vrain Glacier Trail 138
    Coney Lakes Trail 142

Popular Snow Trails 147
    Lefthand Park Reservoir Trail 149
    Waldrop Trails (North and South) 152
    Pawnee Pass Trail 155
    Buchanan Pass Trail via Beaver Reservoir 159
    King Lake Trail 162

Afterword 165
August Evening at Crater Lake by Reg Saner 170
Further Reading 171
Photographic Credits 173
Index 174

to my Mother and Father

REGIONAL MAP

U.S.G.S. 7.5 MINUTE TOPOGRAPHIC MAP INDEX

1. SHADOW MOUNTAIN
2. ISOLATION PEAK
3. ALLENS PARK
4. STRAWBERRY LAKE
5. MONARCH LAKE
6. WARD
7. EAST PORTAL
8. NEDERLAND

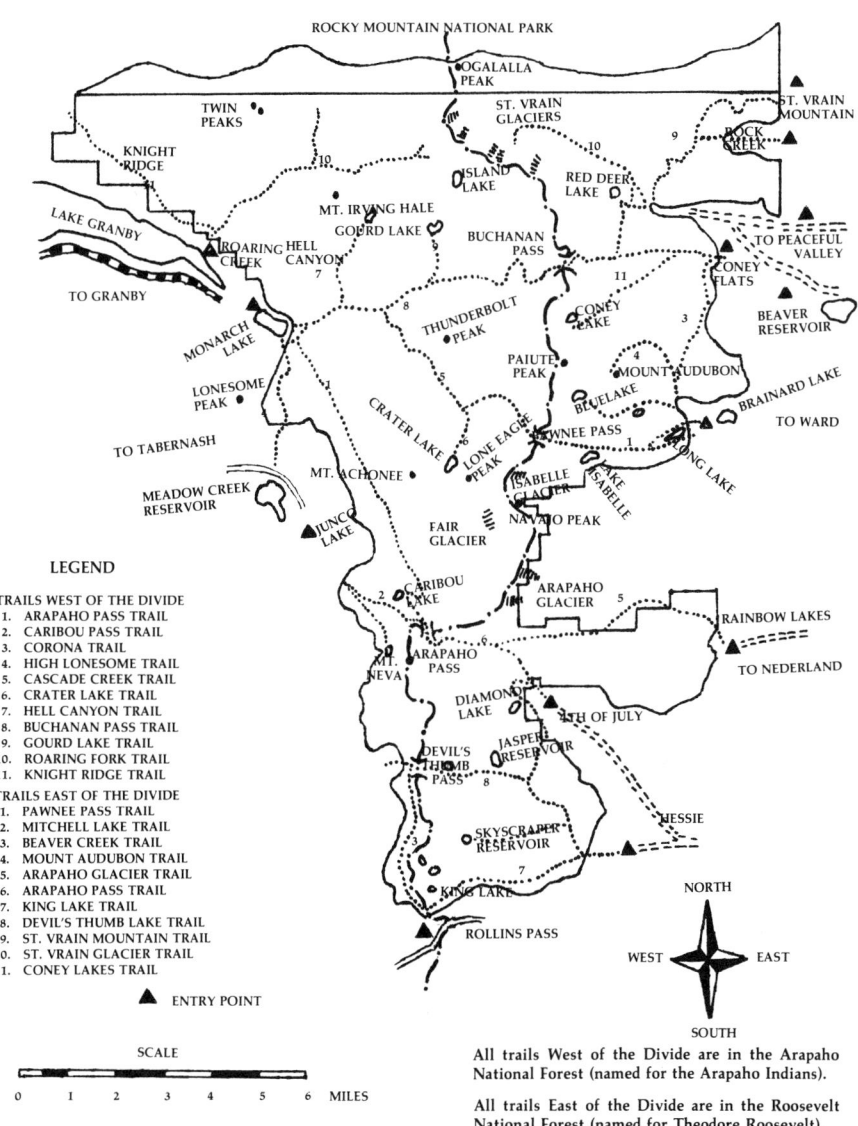

The view from Lake Isabelle will always be safe, thanks to the efforts of U.S. Senator Tim Wirth and others who helped gain wilderness designation for this area. Courtesy Linda Elinoff.

Mount Achonee (12,649 feet), as seen from the headwaters of Arapaho Creek, in late summer. Courtesy Charles W. Murray, Jr.

FOREWORD

Generations to come may look to the period of the 1970s and 1980s not so much for what we as a society built in the physical sense, but rather for how we preserved and protected our precious natural resources. Nowhere is that promise for the future more evident than in those policy considerations surrounding the designation of wilderness areas.

In 1978, the Congress was presented with a special opportunity to preserve one such area in close proximity to the booming Denver-Boulder metropolitan area of Colorado's Front Range. The addition of Indian Peaks to the National Wilderness Preservation System afforded us a chance to protect a unique area—an "urban" wilderness area of pristine alpine lands in stark contrast to the adjoining relaities of our increasingly urban and suburban life-styles.

The development of the Indian Peaks Wilderness Plan by a representative volunteer task force of concerned Coloradans was a wonderful example of effective citizen participation in government. In addition, the many, many months of ensuing negotiations between federal officials, concerned citizens, affected state and local governments, and industry that preceded the designation of Indian Peaks are indicative of the care and concern that all Coloradans have for the protection of this beautiful area. This field guide to Indian Peaks is a natural extension of that concern—helping to educate and guide those unfamiliar with the area and, perhaps more importantly, furthering the process of building an understanding of the area's delicate ecological balance.

Indian Peaks today faces unprecedented demands in terms of use. I sincerely believe that this guide will help to meet that increased demand and to ease its pressures. At a minimum, both goals must continue to guide our efforts so that future generations may find the joy and experiences in Indian Peaks that we now relish.

U.S. Senator Timothy E. Wirth

For a number of years much of my life was spent either in the wilderness or on the borders of the settled country—if, indeed, "settled" is a term that can rightly be applied . . . The free, self-reliant, adventurous life, with its rugged and stalwart democracy; the wild surroundings, the grand beauty of the scenery, the chance to study the ways and habits of the woodland creatures—all these unite to give to (this) career . . . its peculiar charm . . . it cultivates that vigorous manliness for the lack of which in a nation, as in an individual, the possession of no other qualities can possibly atone.

No one, but he who has partaken thereof, can understand the keen delight of (these) lonely lands. For him is the joy of the horse well ridden and the rifle well held; for him the long days of toil and hardship, resolutely endured, and crowned at the end with triumph. In after-years there shall come forever to his mind the memory of endless prairies shimmering in the bright sun; of vast snow-clad wastes lying desolate under gray skies; of the melancholy marshes; of the rush of mighty rivers; of the breath of the evergreen forest in summer; of the crooning of ice-armored pines at the touch of the winds of winter; of cataracts roaring between hoary mountain masses; of all the innumerable sights and sounds of the wilderness; of its immensity and mystery; and of the silences that brood in its still depths.

—Theodore Roosevelt
Sagamore Hill, June, 1893
A Preface to *The Wilderness Hunter*
(G.P. Putnam's Sons, 1895, pp. ix-x)

Acknowledgements

I am not a professional naturalist, and, although all errors of fact are exclusively my own, I should like to acknowledge with sincere gratitude those who assisted me in the preparation of this book.

First, I would like to thank Dr. John Marr, professor emeritus at the University of Colorado at Boulder and former director of the Institute of Artic and Alpine Research, which is adjacent to the wilderness. Dr. Marr graciously gave me permission to use his classic publication "Ecosystems of the East Slope of the Front Range in Colorado" as a source document. This publication is now out of print but was originally published by the University of Colorado in 1967.

Reg Saner, poet/professor at the University of Colorado, was kind enough to grant permission to reprint his poem "August Evening at Crater Lake" in the afterword (from *So This is the Map*, Random House, New York, 1981.

Laurie Rowe, a wildlife conservation officer for the state of Colorado whose patrol district includes a portion of the Indian Peaks, was very helpful in achieving accuracy with respect to wildlife.

Sharon Baker and Morna Scott of the Boulder District Forest Service office were most courteous and made my visits there both pleasant and productive. Many thanks also to Bob Allison, wilderness ranger, who proofread the manuscript, and to Margaret Foster of the Granby office, both of whom supplied slides.

A special note of gratitude to Beverly Noun and Larry Bulling, of then Congressman Tim Wirth's Denver district office, for asistance with the foreword.

Greg Fife, long-time friend and professional geologist, has taught me a great deal about the geology of the Rockies over the years on our many hunting, backpacking, and fishing trips.

Linda Elinoff, my wife, generously donated some of her photographs to illustrate the book, as did my father, Charles William Murray, Jr. Thanks also to Bob Pollock for the cover photo.

I would also like to thank all of those various comrades and companions of the wilderness trail who, over the years, have taught me much about the mountains and man. Some are dead and others are still living. Although their numbers prevent individual mention, they are not forgotten in my heart. To all of them, I here offer my formal thanks.

PREFACE

The wilderness retains the hardship, risk, and challenge that was the essence of primitive America, and that is so much a part of our national experience and character. Although we can no longer cross the continent in the manner of Lewis and Clark, encountering only wild animals and scattered nomadic tribes, or explore whole pristine ranges in the rugged but casual style of Jim Bridger, or roam as freely and proudly as Cochise and Geronimo, it is still possible—remarkably enough—to find sanctuaries of that vanished, primeval America. The need for wilderness has become particularly acute in the last quarter of the twentieth century, with the many stresses of modern life. Traditional families have been scattered across the land through the increased mobility of American society. A renaissance of science and technology has revolutionized our way of life and our outlook on the universe. The city has become, as in no other period in history, the pre-eminent unit of social organization. Men and women now spend their entire adult lives exclusively in urban and suburban areas, separated almost completely from the Earth, and frequently alienated from one another. Mankind also lives under the constant threat of nuclear annihilation. Given all of these factors, there is an urgent need for wilderness areas like the Indian Peaks, particularly when they are closely located to densely populated regions like the Front Range of Colorado.

The conflict arises when the demand for a primitive area exceeds its natural ability to absorb that use, so that the process of recreation results in destruction. Such is the case in the Indian Peaks. No natural community, with the possible exception of the tropical coral reef, is as fragile as that which is predominant in the Indian Peaks: the alpine ecosystem. The extremely small number of plant and animal species, the slow rates of decomposition, and the severe effects of climate all render it uniquely vulnerable to the disruptive influences of man. High lakes can become biologically inactive as a result of acid rain. Mountain streams can become quickly polluted by careless mining, grazing, or lumbering. Subalpine woods can become sterilized by the gathering of deadfall for firewood. And the tundra itself, quickly worn by human steps, is soon infiltrated by needle ice, which leaves the ground unsuitable for revegetation.

Because of this vulnerability and the unacceptable levels of resource damage that began to occur after 1978, when the Indian Peaks was officially designated a wilderness area by President Jimmy Carter, additional administrative measures were instituted to further protect the area. These include the prohibition of campfires and camping in certain watersheds and during specified times of the year; limitations on backcountry horse travel; constraints on parking at major points of access; and the recent requirements of permits for backcountry travel (as is also the case in nearby Rocky Mountain National Park). These steps were taken not to arbitrarily limit the public's freedom, but to make certain that, through proper management, this freedom will still be possible in the next century.

The Indian Peaks Wilderness Area is singular in several respects. First, it is one of the most heavily used wilderness areas in the United States, with 110,000 visitors in 1986. It has become the first wilderness area in the Rocky Mountain region to establish a quota and permit system. It is not inconceivable that this system, if successful, will be implemented in other wilderness areas, particularly in the East, before the decade is over. A small part of the Indian Peaks Wilderness Area actually extends north over the boundary into the national park. Arapaho Glacier, just north of Arapaho Pass, has the distinction of being the southern-most glacier in the Rocky Mountains; and Sawtooth Mountain, just south of Buchanan Pass, is the easternmost point on the Continental Divide. Although the Indian Peaks is a relatively small wilderness area (73,391 acres), only one-sixth the size of the Weminuche, which is the largest in the state, it contains a rich diversity of natural features and forms, and fauna and flora. Included in the Indian Peaks are vast areas of alpine tundra and coniferous sub-alpine forest, numerous cirque basins with remnant glaciers, and nearly fifty lakes, all in the shadows of the Continental Divide. Several rare animal species are found here, including wolverine, Canadian lynx, Shiras moose, and Emerald Lake trout.

This book was written both as a field and trail guide, not to stimulate use, which will occur regardless of any publication, but to enlighten that use. There has always been a need for this book. Now it has been written. But, more importantly, there is a profound need for this wilderness, and for more like it. In a world of hatred and madness, where entire races have been exterminated and lovely cities turned to radioactive ash, where whole societies have been enslaved and irreplaceable genius assasinated, men and women desperately need primitive areas like the Indian Peaks, places where they can step back into time, and see what all of America once was like, or, rather, step out of time, into a timeless realm that existed long before them and that will endure long after them.

As a result of this process, they will hopefully grow to have a more civilized, and not merely artificial, way of life. The mere act of seeking out the wilds is a sign of health, a quiet revolution by the individual against all that threatens to weaken or poison him, the opening of a dialogue between the ephemeral and the eternal. It is a statement, an affirmation, an implicit vow that he will inquire into that process in which all things, including his very nature, are ultimately revealed. The lessons are there, disarming in their simplicity, calming in their final unity. There are the enormous crags, which starkly remind man of his impermanence and underline the necessity of human action. There is the procession of seasons, which restores our faith in the continual creative and healing processes of nature and of life. And there are the myriad laws and shared contracts of the natural world, which bring to mind that inner order of ethical principles to which the individual must always remain faithful, as well as those compacts to be honored with society, government, and humanity.

The Indian Peaks offer people a place where they might return to their origins, to nature, and to the wilds; a place to escape all that threatens to dehumanize and impoverish them; a place to restore their equilibrium and their ability to cope with life. There was a time not so very long ago when all of the North American continent lay before us as rough and untamed as the Indian Peaks. Now we have only a few refuges of that once vast wilderness left. These sanctuaries will always remain, fortunately, so that our distant ancestors might go there and grasp the very special birthright of this nation, its great frontier tradition, the democratic challenge that drew people from all over the world to its shores, and continues to do so. And, of course, so much more. And who knows but that one day our descendents may steal among the stars, on engines that comprehend the very science of the universe, a billion miles through deepest space, to find the simple truths that can be discovered in places like the Indian Peaks?

PART I
The Natural History

I climbed alone over huge rocks, loosely poised, a mile or more, still edging towards the clouds...the mountain seemed a vast aggregation of loose rocks, as if some time it had rained rocks, and they lay as they fell on the mountain sides, nowhere fairly at rest, but leaning on each other....They were the raw materials of a planet dropped from an unseen quarry, which the vast chemistry of nature would anon work up, or work down, into the smiling and verdant plains of Earth....Occasionally I caught sight of a dark, damp crag....It reminded me of the creations of the old epic and dramatic poets, of Atlas, Vulcan, the Cyclops, and Prometheus. Such was the Caucacus and the rock where Prometheus was bound. Aechylus had no doubt visited such scenery as this....It was vast, titanic, and such as men never inhabit. The tops of the mountains are among the unfinished parts of the globe, whither it is a slight insult to the gods to climb and pry into their secrets, and try their effect on our humanity....Only daring and insolent men, perchance, go there....Nature was here something savage, and awful, though beautiful. This was the Earth of which we have heard, made out of Chaos and Old Night. Here was no man's garden. It was not lawn, nor pasture, nor mead, nor woodland, nor lea, nor arable, nor waste land. It was the fresh and natural surface of the planet Earth, as it was made forever and ever. It was matter, vast, terrific...The home, this, of Necessity and Fate. There was clearly felt the presence of a force not bound to be kind to man. It was a place for heathenism and superstitious rites....We walked over it with a certain Awe.

Henry David Thoreau
Ktaadn
1864

ARCHAEOLOGY AND HUMAN HISTORY

Man first came to the New World tens of thousands of years ago across a land bridge that extended between present-day Alaska and Siberia during periods of glacial inactivity. Aboriginal populations probably visited the Indian Peaks as recently as 20,000 years ago. At that time what is today the Great Basin—the cold desert between the Rockies and the Sierra Nevadas—was a fertile land of lakes, in which many extinct species such as camels, wooly mammoths, and saber-toothed tigers lived. Various human communities existed across North America, but because of the paucity of sites in the Indian Peaks, it is difficult to construct an accurate picture of what form that took locally. It is clear that by at least 11,000 years ago these people regularly crossed the same passes that are used by backcountry travelers today.

More recently, the Ute, Cheyenne, and Arapaho tribes used the area for hunting and for travel to the Western Slope. Kiowa and Comanche were present to a lesser degree. The first Europeans to enter the state of Colorado were Spaniards, who explored north from the city of Santa Fe in the early 1700s. Most of their activities were concentrated in the San Juans, where they searched for gold and silver. In 1776, when Jefferson was writing the Declaration of Independence in Philadelphia, two Franciscan priests, Escalante and Dominguez, were exploring deep into the wilderness of southern Colorado, giving names to many of the passes, rivers, and peaks which remain today. Unless one believes stories of Viking petroglyphs in Western Slope caves, no white man had yet seen the Front Range of Colorado.

In 1803, France sold to the United States a huge territory between the Mississippi River and the Rocky Mountains, essentially the drainage of the Missouri River. Even before the signing of the Louisiana Purchase, President Jefferson had directed his personal secretary, Meriwether Lewis, and William Clark to lead an expedition up the Missouri and find a route to the Pacific Ocean. Practically nothing was known of the interior of America, and only a vague idea existed of the Rocky Mountains. The hope was to find a short portage that would lead over the mountains from the headwaters of the Missouri to the headwaters of the Columbia, which had been discovered earlier by Captain Robert Gray and named for his ship, the *Columbia*. The expedition passed a few hundred miles to the north of the Indian Peaks in 1805. Several years later, the Pike Expedition entered Colorado.

The expedition of Lewis and Clark initiated the great age of trapping, when the first mountain men, who trapped beaver and other furbearers, began to actively pursue their profession in the Rocky Mountains. Sometime in the early nineteenth century, the first trappers entered Colorado and the Front Range from the north, men mostly of French descent. The first rendezvous was held in 1825 on the Green River in Wyoming, and the last was held in 1840. A rendezvous lasted about three weeks and was far more than simply an exchange of furs for supplies. It was a social event and an opportunity for the men to share new information about the vast wilderness being explored.

After fifteen years, the price of fur fell as beaver hats went out of fashion, and the age of mountain men quickly receded into the chronicles of history. For a short time, a small group of men had lived one of the most exciting and exacting lives the country has known. Most are forgotten, but many of these pioneers live on in our folklore and in the place names of the West—names like Bridger, Sublette, Colter, Astor, and Bonneville. With their Hawken rifles, double-ought traps, and painted horses, they were the first white men to explore this vast wilderness and the last to ever see it true wilderness again.

In 1839, as the initial phase of exploration declined, two Frenchmen, the St. Vrain brothers, entered Colorado from the south and, in partnership with the Bent brothers, built Fort St. Vrain on the South Platte River, today the site of a nuclear reactor. Trading with luminaries like Kit Carson and the southern Cheyenne and Arapaho, they began a flourishing retail business. Trade soon extended southward to Taos and Santa Fe. People began to settle in Colorado; the great age of emigration and colonization had begun. So popular and successful were the St. Vrain brothers that their names, too, became a part of history. The major drainage on the eastern slope of the Indian Peaks is named for them, as well as the nuclear plant.

While trappers needed character and honesty to stay alive in Indian Territory, the U.S. Cavalry did not. Next to slavery, the Indian wars were probably the saddest and darkest chapter in our nation's history. One hundred years after the signing of the Declaration of Independence, the last heroic act of resistance on the part of the Great Plains tribes occurred at the Battle of the Little Bighorn in what is today Montana. A few years earlier, most of the peaceful Arapaho and Cheyenne of Colorado had been massacred by the Colorado militia at Sand Creek. The survivors, mostly Arapaho, were sent to a reservation in the Wind River Mountains, where they remain today. The Mountain Utes live on a reservation in southern Colorado.

Scientific explorations then began to enter the West, led by now famous men like Fremont, Powell, King, Wheeler, and Hayden. They made many discoveries, including that of precious metals in the Rocky Mountains. On January 15, 1859, gold was discovered in Gold Hill, not far from the present eastern border of the Indian Peaks Wilderness, and for the next several decades a "boom and bust" cycle of mining characterized life in Boulder County and elsewhere in Colorado. Twenty-eight mining, logging, and supply camps were built in the county, only half of which remain today as scattered settlements and towns. Two railroads were constructed in this period and then abandoned. As the mineral resources were depleted, logging and then cattle ranching began to dominate the local economy. Many old crumbled and decayed cabins used by the ranchers and cowboys as summer homes can still be found in or near the wilderness area.

One of the more prominent historical sites in the wilderness area is Rollins Pass, constructed in 1905 and used for twenty-four years as the main line of the Moffat Railroad (the Needle's Eye Tunnel, 2.9 miles from the summit, caved in and has been closed since 1980). A brochure offering a self-guided tour is available in the Boulder district office of the forest service. The Switzerland Trail, now county roads 118, 93, and 120, is an old railroad grade which formerly connected Boulder with camps in Ward, Eldora, and elsewhere. In 1919 a flash flood wiped out the line in Four Mile Canyon. A classic example of the extremes to which prospectors will go can be found in the Fourth of July mine, 5.5 miles west of Eldora on county road 111. The mine is halfway up a route over the divide and is situated in the windswept krummholz against the flank of South Arapaho Peak. Six miles west of Peaceful Valley are the remnants of the Middle St. Vrain logging camp.

Red Indian Paintbrush with purple aster and yellow goldeneye. Courtesy Charles W. Murray, Jr.

FAUNA AND FLORA

The Indian Peaks Wilderness area is the home of many plants and animals commonly found in the Rocky Mountains. Because of pressures from civilization, four mammal species recently present are now extinct in this region—the grizzly bear, the timber wolf, the otter, and the mountain goat. Travelers should avoid picking wild flowers because many of them are quite rare (such as the calypso orchid), and a few seasons of picking could render them extinct as well. Reptiles are not present in the Indian Peaks except perhaps on the Western Slope, where a few lizards can sometimes be seen above Monarch Lake. There have been no sightings of rattlesnakes. Frogs and toads are present, some at surprisingly high elevations.

MAMMALS

The most common large mammal in the wilderness is the mule deer, which can be found from the lower forests to the highest alpine ridges. They are easily distinguished by their sleek grey to brown bodies, their big ears (for which they are named), and the large branched antlers on the bucks. Adults normally weigh between 200 and 300 pounds. The bucks shed their antlers in January and February each year. A few weeks later they begin to grow their new antlers, which are encased in velvet. The velvet is rubbed off against branches after the antlers have turned to bone. The antlers are used by the bucks in shows of prowess during the rut, which occurs in mid-November when the does are fertile. Fawns are born in May and June.

Deer are browsers, feeding on a diet of sagebrush, bitterbrush, mountain mahogany, serviceberry, and other similar plant species. They are most active around dawn and dusk. During the summer the deer separate by sex, with the bucks gathering in the high peaks in friendly bachelor herds and the does keeping pretty much to the lower valleys, where they raise the young.

Elk, or wapiti, are more secretive than mule deer and tend to inhabit more rugged and remote country in the Indian Peaks, such as Hell's Canyon, Wheeler Basin, Roaring Fork Canyon, Upper Cascade Creek, and Upper Buchanan Creek. They are considerably heavier than the mule deer, weighing between 400 and 1,000 pounds. Their bodies are brownish grey, and they have a chestnut mane on their shoulders and neck, a white-yellow rump, and a short trail. The bulls grow antlers that sometimes weigh as much as thirty pounds apiece. The elk's musky scent is very powerful and unmistakable in the deep woods to those who are familiar with it. Elk tracks, like those of the deer, are cloven and elongated and are generally twice as large, averaging four inches in length.

The rut occurs in early fall, usually in September, and the bulls make a peculiar high-pitched whistling sound as they challenge one another. Elk signs most often encountered in the high country include their large wallows, found in swampy areas; their droppings, seen often on the trails; their rub marks on tree trunks; and their enormous day beds, usually an oblong area of crushed grass give or six long. Elk are grazers, feeding primarily on grass, but they will also feed on the brush diet of mule deer, including snowberry. Both deer and elk migrate into lower terrain during the winter.

Transplanted into the Willow Creek Pass area several years ago, the Shiras or Yellowstone moose are now found on the Western Slope of the Indian Peaks. Moose are as large as or larger than elk and are uniformly dark brown or black. The bulls have enormous scoop-shoveled horns. Both sexes have "bells" hanging from their jaws, massive shoulders, and a peculiar curved-down nose. They forage on willow, aspen, red maple, and small brush in the marshlands around rivers, streams, and lakes. Unlike deer and elk, moose can be dangerous and should be left alone.

A rare visitor to the Indian Peaks from established herds to the north and south is the official state animal, the Rocky Mountain bighorn sheep. Sheep inhabit only the very roughest terrain but are built for it, having chunky, muscular bodies. The rams grow massive horns that are never shed and that are used in aggressive displays during the mating season (which corresponds with that of deer, elk, and moose). Ewes have less massive horns than rams. Body color is brown to grey with a light belly, a white rump, and a white muzzle and eye patch.

Black bears are found throughout the wilderness in good numbers. Their primary color phase is cinnamon, although a few specimens are black. Adult bears weigh from 350 to 600 pounds and are omnivorous, feeding on grass, sedges, roots, buds, berries, fruits, honey, insects, and all forms of fresh and decayed meat. In the winter they hibernate, usually at about the 9,000-foot level on the north side of the mountain so that by the time the snows leave their den the country will be warm and food will be plentiful. The cubs—usually twins—are born in mid-winter and stay with the female the second winter in her den. Bears are

Beaver ponds, such as these on the Upper Cascade Creek drainage, are found throughout the wilderness. Courtesy Charles W. Murray, Jr.

nocturnal creatures and are rarely seen. Shy and secretive, they prefer remote side canyons, swamps, and heavily forested slopes. Their familiar tracks, droppings, wallows, and scratch trees can often be found to those who venture a few hundred yards from the trails. All bears, even small ones, should be left alone. The only grizzly bears in Colorado are found in the South San Juan Wilderness, where several years ago an adult female attacked and seriously mauled a bowhunter.

Also found in good numbers in the wilderness are mountain lions, called by some puma or cougars. Adults are grey, have an extremely long tail, and weigh up to 275 pounds. Their tracks are like those of a common house cat, though much larger. Even more reclusive than bears, the lions are rarely, if ever, seen. They breed at any time of the year, with the female bearing two to three kittens that are tawny and black-spotted. Basically a solitary animal, the mountain lion's domain is quite large, averaging fifteen to twenty square miles. Like the bear and coyote, they mark trails, trees, and boulders in a territorial fashion.

Other predators in the Indian Peaks include coyotes, wolverines, lynx, bobcats, pine martens, mink, red and grey foxes, badgers, weasels, and skunks. Above timberline people often see marmots and coneys (or pikas), both of which make squeaking sounds like guinea pigs. On the lower streams, beaver and muskrat can often be observed, and, in the surrounding forests, squirrel, gophers, rabbits, mice, voles, porcupines, raccoons, shrews, bats, and chipmunks can be seen.

BIRDS

A variety of birds can be found in the Indian Peaks, from the tiny broad-tailed hummingbird that winters in Costa Rica to the great horned owl, who lives here year-round. Along streams, people frequently see the ouzel, or water-dipper, a favorite of John Muir, cheerfully fishing for small insects in the shallows. In the summer, many migratory songbirds inhabit these mountains, including the rosy finch, the solitary vireo, the goldfinch, the mountain bluebird, and various orioles and warblers. In cliff areas, the violet-green swallows are always fun to observe. The blue and sharptailed grouse can be seen in the conifer forests, as well as the downy and hairy woodpeckers. Above timberline, ptarmigan are frequently seen and can be easily approached. Occasionally, golden eagles and red-tailed hawks are visible riding the summer thermals. Ravens are populous, as are stellar's jays, along with the common gray jay, known affectionately to all wilderness travelers as the "camp robber."

FISH

The waters of the Indian Peaks have native trout (cutthroat), rainbow trout, brook trout, and limited numbers of brown trout. The native trout were the only fish found in the cold higher waters of the Rockies when the first white men arrived. The brook trout was originally a native to the eastern United States and the rainbow trout to West Coast streams, while the brown trout was transplanted from Europe in 1883.

In the Indian Peaks, the native trout occupy the high lakes and the upper parts of stream drainages. They are not usually found at lower elevations because they do not compete well with brook and rainbow trout. Brook trout prefer the lesser streams and lakes, although they can be found virtually anywhere. Some extremely large brook trout are occasionally taken from the major drainages.

Unlike the others, brook trout spawn in the fall. Rainbow trout have the unique ability to leap when hooked, and their spectacular gameness—which results in hard fights, swift runs, and sudden leaps—makes them a favorite with anglers. The Emerald Lake cutthroat trout is now found in the Indian Peaks, recently transplanted from Emerald Lake in the Weminuche Wilderness to the St. Vrain drainage.

WILDFLOWERS

The first flower to appear after the snow is gone is the snowdrop, followed (at lower elevations in boggy places) by the yellow and dogtooth violet, the white globeflower, and the marsh marigold. Soon thereafter, as the earth begins to warm, an explosion of wild flowers occurs, including spring beauty, bluebell, wild lily-of-the-valley, death camas, buttercup, and numerous others. As the summer progresses, the state flower, the blue columbine, can be found in cool damp places among the rocks along with Indian paintbrush, avalanche lily, purple larkspur, wild iris, shooting star, and a variety of daisies and meadow flowers.

At higher elevations, in the vicinity of decayed logs, the rare calypso orchid can be found, as well as the delicate blue

Black-eyed Susans are found in the aspen groves and lower meadows of the wilderness. Courtesy Linda Elinoff.

harebell, monkeyflower, lupine, scarlet gilia, and yellow arnica. On the tundra, a vast profusion of liliputian flowers can be found, such as miniature violets, tiny cushions of phlox, dwarfed sunflowers, pink moss campion, and forget-me-nots. Many of these flowers are endangered, so it is important not to pick or harm them.

TREES

At lower elevations on the western slope, ponderosa pine, Douglas fir, and white fir are found. Above 9,000 feet, conifers such as the blue spruce, which is the state tree, the Douglas fir, the limber pine, and the lodgepole pine dominate. Occasionally groves of white-trunked aspen trees can be found. A deciduous tree related to the eastern birch and filling the same ecological niche, the aspen is also known as the "quaking aspen" because of the soft, pleasant sound its leaves make as they shimmer and shake with the slightest breeze. Aspens are normally found on sunny southern slopes and open meadows. They also become "nurse" trees for the conifers after a burn. Between 10,500 feet and timberline, the dark timber takes over in uniform and tightly packed stands. Subalpine fir is found, as is corkbark fir, growing side by side with the large specimens of Douglas fir and Colorado blue spruce. At timberline, cold temperatures and winds stunt the trees and cause them to become deformed and to grow close to the ground, resembling bushes. Some species of bristlecone pine found at timberline are very ancient and predate the birth of Christ. They should never be disturbed.

GEOMORPHOLOGY AND GEOGRAPHY

The Indian Peaks is a section of the Continental Divide that runs along the Front Range of Colorado, bounded on the east by the Great Plains and on the west by a large inter-montane park. The north-to-south distance through the peaks is approximately sixteen miles as the crow flies, from the southern boundary of Rocky Mountain National Park to Rollins Pass.

Many geomorphic processes have been active in developing the surface forms of the region, which was uplifted some 135 million years ago. Consequently, there is no single dominant topographic feature for the range as a whole; valleys vary from deep and narrow to shallow and broad, some interstream uplands are knife-edges while others are a broad, gently rolling surface; some high peaks have broad, rounded tops, while others are sharp, with only a few square yards on their summit.[1] The prevalent rocks are Precambrian granites and metamorphics in large batholithic masses and Tertiary quartz that occurs in part as stocks, dikes, and sills injected into the Precambrian rock. A complex pattern of faults has affected topography in many parts of the area, but the most dominant factor in

---

1. Dr. John W. Marr, *Ecosystems of the East Slope of the Front Range in Colorado* (Boulder: University of Colorado, 1967), p. 19.

determining the modern appearance of the Indian Peaks is glacial activity, which produced the now spectacular landscapes of the higher areas and influenced topography all the way down to 8,000 feet. Eastward and westward from the divide, the topography becomes progressively less spactacular as the effects of the valley glaciers diminish.

The major valleys have the broad U-shaped cross-section profile and the giant-step longitudinal profile characteristic of glacial valleys, and they terminate in glacial cirques whose cliffs may be as high as a fifty-story skyscraper. Some of these cirques are over a mile wide. There are many hanging valleys, talus slopes, and remnant glaciers in the rock. Gentle valley slopes and broad ridge tops have very nearly always been terraced into broad steps by solifluction, which is a geographic effect of the permafrost resulting from the creeping of thawed soil over the frozen ground beneath. Other factors influencing the surface of the ground in the upper valleys above timberline include frost heaving and boiling and the frequent freeze-thaw cycles of soil water. Over the ages, these have produced a variety of polygons, stripes, frost boils, and other forms of "patterned" ground.

Small moraines occur near the front of current glaciers in the heads of some valleys and sometimes form the dam for a small lake. Most valleys, as in the upper St. Vrain drainage, have a long series of lakes, each one resulting from one of the glacier-produced steps. As glaciers entered the wider valley, they usually did not spread out and fill the entire valley. Rather, they maintained the dimensions of the upper valley and produced giant lateral moraines that dammed up drainage from surrounding slopes and valleys, resulting in boggy subalpine areas. Some locations, such as the top and east end of Niwot Ridge, were apparently never touched by glaciation.[2]

Glaciers have had a profound effect on the geology and

---

2. *Ibid.*, p. 53

ecology of the region. As we are currently in what most authorities agree is an interglacial period, the glaciers have temporarily retreated to the highest and most protected areas of the Indian Peaks. They can be seen in the country north of Buchanan Pass and south of Pawnee Pass in the upper St. Vrain drainage.

Glaciation is apparently a result of a complex cycle of heating and cooling in the Earth's biosphere, and this cycle may be a result of the internal dynamics of the land, sea, and air, as well as the activity of the sun. When the climate begins to cool again, as it has several times in the recent past, then glaciers will once again begin to physically alter the appearance and life of these high mountains.

CLIMATOLOGY

The climate of the Indian Peaks is continental, with Pacific air masses entering the range from the west and Gulf air masses from the southeast. The former often result in the extremely strong winds for which Boulder County is famous and usually produce the familiar giant "crest-cloud" along the crest of the Divide—a silvery cloud that resembles the large mother ship of science fiction lore. These winds can also produce significant precipitation at higher elevations.

Gulf air masses, most evident in the spring and fall, give rise to the major precipitation on the East Slope. Cold fronts from Canada can arise any time of the year and often move southward parallel to the mountains, forming stratus clouds at the base of the warm air they are forcing upward and pouring cold air back into the mountain valleys. The local consequence is a temperature inversion with warm, sunny weather above and gloomy, colder weather below. When one of these northern air masses converges with a Gulf front, large amounts of precipitation can result. Summer convectional storms are frequent, occurring almost every day in some years.

Seasonally, the climate in the Indian Peaks is basically cold and moist. Summers are short, cool, and moist with many late-lying snowbanks and frequent thunderstorms. Hot days are infrequent, whereas cool, wet intervals of a few days are common. Autumn is dry, usually cool during the day and often cold at night. At least one snowstorm usually initiates or breaks into the brief Indian summer, and on rare occasions it delivers several feet of snow. There are also many intervals of clear, calm, hot days and cool nights; winds are strong at times. The winter is long, cold, and windy and usually produces an abundance of snow. The spring is short, cool, and wet; in most years, at least one spring storm yields two or more feet of snow. Deep snow lingers long in the subalpine forest, sometimes far into summer. Prevailing winds are always from the west. East winds are more gentle, often producing heavy fog in any season. Winds from either the east or west can result in precipitation.[3]

---

3. *Ibid.*, p. 27.

THE UPPER MONTANE FOREST

The predominant ecosystems of the Indian Peaks are the subalpine and the alpine. The upper montane forest, located between the lower montane and the subalpine, is found only on the Western Slope of the wilderness in the lower Buchanan and Arapaho Creek drainages. This ecosystem is also referred to as the Douglas fir zone or the Douglas fir climax zone. As the name implies, the role of the Douglas fir is distinctive. Slender lodgepole pine and aspen sometimes infiltrate these areas, as staging and transition into the subalpine is occurring. Occasionally, the Colorado blue spruce is also found at these lower elevations.

Near the confluence of the two streams with Monarch Lake, dense aquatic shrub communities are found. This is classic moose habitat. Some of these communities are ten feet tall and are so dense as to preclude cross-country travel. Both willow and birch grow here. Raspberry bushes are found on south-facing slopes around and above Monarch Lake. These lower elevations are a favored summer range for the female deer and elk. Bear also enjoy the shady seclusion of these dense forests and the profusion of food in the form of roots, leaves, and berries.

THE SUBALPINE FOREST

The subalpine forest lies above the upper montane forest and below the alpine tundra. It is also referred to as the spruce-fir climax region or the Canadian/Hudsonian zone. Conditions in this area are comparable with those found in the far north, where trees thin out and become dwarfed at the southern fringes of the arctic tundra. In the Indian Peaks, this region is between approximately 9,300 and 11,000 feet, cutting across the lowermost of the conspicuous glacial cirques. A more or less homogenous, simple, and continuous vegetation occurs at intermediate altitudes in this region, while higher and lower elevations support complex and heterogenous vegetation.[4] These transition zones between various stands are called ecotones, and many species may be more numerous here than in the mature heart of a fixed community.

In the central area, dense evergreen forests of spire-crowned spruce and fir trees stretch across valleys and over ridges for miles and miles, broken only by streams, chains of small lakes, meadowlands, and stands of broad-crowned limber pine on the more exposed ridge tops. The forest is often primeval and has changed little for many hundreds, if not thousands, of years. Some individual specimens of Englemann spruce and subalpine fir are among the largest in the region, attaining heights of one hundred or more feet and diameters of three feet or more.

---

4. *Ibid.*, p. 55

Small ponds such as this one sometimes form in the subalpine forest. Courtesy Charles W. Murray, Jr.

The rugged and remote character of the terrain, as well as the boulderly substratum and the relatively low timber values, have saved these forests from commercial exploitation.

The lower elevations are predominated by lodgepole pine and aspen groves, with a few stands of spruce-fir. Travelers will notice that many of the aspens (such as those along the road toward Brainard Lake) are curiously deformed, with trunks that assume shapes ressembling dog legs, S-curves, elbows, and knees. The deformity occurs in the lower part of the trunk, four or five feet from the ground. Above this level, the smooth white trunks assume the normal immaculate attitude of the aspens. This results from the compressive and creeping effects of the massive snowdrifts that linger through May and June, overlapping with the beginning of seasonal growth. Sometimes you can also detect where hungry elk have eaten away at the bark in particularly bad years. Aspens are also popular trees for bears to mark with their claws. In this lower zone of the subalpine, wet meadows are common, particularly in areas of high water table. Dry meadows or "elk parks" often occur on valley slopes and ridges.

The upper elevations are dominated by the spruce and fir. Many generations of trees have lived, died, and fallen over in these long-persisting stands, and wind-throw of both living and dead trees is common. The resulting tangle of stumps and fallen logs in all stages of decay creates the confusing jungle referred to as "down timber" or "dark timber." It is here that elk are most numerous—and least accessible. These old spruce-fir stands are relatively stable in character, changing very little from century to century. As the older trees die, seedlings or suppressed saplings grow rapidly to form replacements that keep the stand relatively closed. Because of the dense growth and thick canopy, the forest floor is heavily shaded, making it difficult for other species, particularly shrubs, to infiltrate the stand. Occasionally, blueberry bushes can be found.

Wet, marshy soils surrounding the abundant glacial lakes in the Indian Peaks provide a suitable environment for extensive shrub communities.[5] Several species of willow and dwarf birch produce a very dense community through which passage is extremely difficult. These are successional stands in most cases, reclaiming area that was under water in the past. The shrubs are excellent windbreaks and cause a deep accumulation of snow (as do all the forests and communities of the subalpine region), resulting in stored precipitation for the summer. Average precipitation throughout the Indian Peaks is thirty water inches per year.

---

5. *Ibid.*, p. 56.

THE ALPINE TUNDRA

The alpine tundra begins where the treeline ends. In the Indian Peaks, this generally occurs about 11,400 feet but varies depending on location. The last trees are known as "krummholz," which comes from the German meaning "elfintimber" or "crooked wood." This final band of coniferous trees is dwarfed and deformed by exposure, many times with a finely crafted bonsai-like appearance. Frequently, the branches of the trees grow in opposite direction of the prevailing north-westerly winds, pointing toward the south-southeast as surely as a compass.

Above timberline there is a complete absence of all upright trees and tall shrubs. Nothing but arctic vegetation can grow, producing the familiar "barren" appearance of the tundra. In fact, the word tundra comes from the Russian, meaning "land of no trees." In Finnish, the word "tunturi" means arctic or barren hill, and in Lapp, "tundar" refers to a marshy place. In any language, tundra is a realm beyond the trees, an austere and strangely beautiful zone, the final place on Earth before the sun and moon and stars.

Although tundra vegetation appears homogenous, the patterns and communities are actually quite complex, reflecting the influences of exposure, soil, macro and micro climate, landforms, and various physical events.[6] The actual number of plant and animal species is unusually low.

---

6. *Ibid.*, p. 79.

The tundra is a harsh and unforgiving environment in which no trees or upright shrubs are found. Photograph taken at 12,100 feet on the east side of Pawnee Pass looking south. Courtesy Linda Elinoff.

A number of theories have been advanced to explain this lack of species diversity, including spatial heterogeneity, climatic stability, competition and predation, evolution, and severity of climate. There is as yet, however, no consensus on this subject among authorities, as there is yet no unified theory on the origin of the Rocky Mountains. Whatever the cause, each organism in this very specialized community occupies a particular functional niche, analogous to the particular job a single human being might have in human society. Where in human society we have the flow of money which facilitates the transfer of goods and services and thus sustains the population, in these natural communities we have the flow of energy from the sun through the autotrophic communities (plants), where the energy is initially captured through photosynthesis, to the heterotrophic component (the animals, including herbivores and carnivores). All food chains end with the decomposers—organisms that reduce plants and animals into the simplest substances available again for the food chain.

The alpine tundra has many unique features. First, as a result of geology and climate, it has a compressed growing and reproductive season. Most of the vegetation is, consequently, perennial, and most of the animal life has either long periods of dormancy or strong migratory habits. Plants have many adaptive differences from their lower counterparts, including lower temperatures, higher photosynthetic rates, and, of course, their actual physical appearance.

Throughout the tundra, cushion and mat-forming plants are important. Low and hugging to the ground, they are better able to withstand the climate and are more resistant to desiccation in the epidermal hairs and scales, which also reflect the sunlight. These plants provide a microclimate which harbors some invertebrate life (like snails) and insects (including black flies, deer flies, bumblebees, butterflies, beetles, and mosquitoes). Animals most common are rodents, such as snowshoe hares, mice, and marmots, and migratory ungulates like sheep, deer, and elk. Ptarmigan are found year-round on the tundra, as are weasels.

Where the ground is low and moist, there are frequently bogs whose anaerobic conditions suspend decay and whose acid waters are dark brown. In higher, drier areas, vegetation is scant and the ground is bare, taking on the appearance of a rock field. These are called "fellfields," an anglicization of the Danish "fjoeld-mark," or rock desert. Many of these rocks have lichens on them, a primitive form of life that is actually an algae and a fungus in a symbiotic relationship. Cotton grass generally dominates the tundra, but some areas have luxurious shrubs, grasses, and legumes. Often, colorful flowers mingle with the dominant plants, all of miniature size.

Pockets of heavy snow create two types of habitats: the snowpatch and the snow bed. The snow patch occurs where wind-driven snow collects in shallow depressions and protects the plants beneath. This condition is conducive to growing willow, birch, and heath. Snow beds occur where large masses of snow protect the plants, and as the snow melts, it provides a continuous supply of water. Sedges, hairgrasses, mosses, and even willows may appear here.

Scientists have identified ten major stand types in the Indian Peaks alpine ecosystem: the **Kobresia meadow**, which takes on a beautiful golden hue in the autumn; the **Hairgrass meadow**, which is the best development of a true grass meadow at these elevations; the **Parry's clover meadow**, a fragrant pink flower that grows in shallow areas that fill with snow during the winter; the **Adoneus buttercup stand**, (especially conspicuous in the early summer), whose brilliant yellow flowers often appear against a background layer of thin rotten snow; the **Snowbank complex**, which is a moist area that fosters the growth of lush sedges and grasses; the **Cushion plant stand**, which occurs in places exposed to severe desiccation year-round and includes moss campion, sandwort, and alpine forget-me-not; the **Dryas stand**, which occurs on gentle slope areas and produces small flowered terraces; the **Sedge-Grass Wet-Meadow stand**, which is a lush meadow that grows on solifluction terraces where the humus soil is kept wet or moist all summer by groundwater; the **Willow-Sedge hummock stand**, which has a low slope gradient that is dominated by hummocky topography; and the **Tundra Valley stands**, which vary from place to place but may include spruce and fir tree islands above timberline in the lee of boulders, as well as marshy areas where willow, labrador tea, sphagnum, and blueberry dominate.[7]

Geology and climate have had a profound influence on the ecology of the tundra. Most valleys in the region have precipitous slopes, abundant lakes and snowfields, some glacially polished bedrock surfaces, rounded rock knolls sculpted by glacial ice, an occasional boulder left perched on smaller stones by melting glacial ice, and talus slides.

---

7. *Ibid.*, p. 81.

Uplands include gently rolling surfaces that end abruptly at the foot of steep, jagged ridges or at the edge of cliffs and canyons hundreds of feet high. In such a harsh and unforgiving zone, something as insignificant as the activity of the pocket gopher becomes a powerful force on the vegetation, as it burrows and disrupts the soil. The activities of man, even those that are apparently innocent, are even more insidious and destructive and can alter conditions for centuries.

PART II
Backcountry Travel

I with great difficulty prosued. . .to the top of the mountain where I found the snow from 12 to 15 feet deep. . .here was Winter with all it's rigors; the air was cold my hand and feet were benumed. , .if we proceeded and Should git bewildered in those Mountains the certainty was that we should lose all of our horses and consequently our baggage estrements perhaps our papers and thus eventually resque the loss of our discoveries which we had already made if we should be so fortunate as to escape with life. . .we therefore come to the resolution to return with our horses while they were yet strong and in good order, and indeavor to keep them so untill we could precure an indian to conduct us over the Snowey Mountains.

—Captain Meriwether Lewis, Tuesday, June 17th, 1806 from an entry in his journal on the expedition to the west, while attempting to cross the Bitterroot Range in the vicinity of Lolo Pass.

WEATHER

Essentially, there are two seasons in the high country: winter, which lasts from approximately October 1 to June 1, and summer, which normally begins in early June at the lower elevations and lingers on into the final weeks of September. Even during the summer, though, it is possible to have freezing temperatures and sudden snow squalls, particularly at the higher elevations. Winter is long and brutal. Above 9,000 feet, there is virtually no spring or fall as they are known and enjoyed in other regions of the country.

JUNE

Most of the major trails at lower elevations are snow-free by June 15. Mild winters have seen the higher trails open (though not in fine shape) by early June. After hard winters, it has been difficult to get above 10,000 feet until July 4 or later.

High water on the streams is a major obstacle to travel in June. As the streams drain the snowfall of the preceding winter, they swell to three or four times their normal flow. June is usually a month of fairly low precipitation and mild weather. The days gradually become warmer as July nears. Summer crowds don't really start until later in the month.

The wild flowers begin to blossom below timberline, and waterfalls are at the peak of their beauty. The elk and deer begin moving into their summer range. Fawns and calves are born in remote canyons and forests. But the weather is unpredictable. Some years it is memorable. Other years it is quite forgetable. Because of the melting snow, the trails are often as wet and muddy as those in a tropical rainforest, making foot travel less than pleasant.

JULY

When the water begins to lower in early July and the ice begins to melt off the high lakes, fishing in the Indian Peaks is at its best. Stirred to activity by the long sunny days and warming water, trout go into fantastic feeding binges, sometimes leaping several feet into the air to catch a particular morsel. Wild flowers are universally at their prime as the last of the snow begins to melt. The elk and deer are finally and fully on their summer range.

July is also the month when the troublesome mosquitoes wake up. There are usually clouds of them around bogs, meadows, and lakes—anyplace where the snow has just melted. Ticks and chiggers are not much of a problem in the Indian Peaks because of the elevation. Some may be encountered around lower Buchanan and Arapaho creeks because of the frequent horse traffic.

Usually within several days either side of the Fourth of July, the summer thunderstorms begin, appearing with regularity every afternoon. Extended rainy periods, while infrequent, indicate the presence of a stalled frontal system. This is the warmest month of all, with temperatures in the eighties, even at higher elevations, and nights dropping down only into the low forties or upper thirties. By the end of July, stream and lake temperatures have reached their maximum for the year. Also by the end of July, the maximum biomass for the ecosystem has been attained. Biomass is the living weight of a specified region, that is, the amount of organic matter produced by photosynthesis, usually expressed in calories or grams per meter. Naturally this varies seasonally and by altitude and latitude and culminates sometime after the longest day of the year.

AUGUST

Beginning about the middle of August, daily temperatures drop and a faint chill, portending the inevitable approach of winter, is often in the morning air. The weather can be unpredictable. If the weather is mild and not rainy, August can be a prime month for backpacking excursions. Crowds begin to thin out as families return to the city and students go back to college. The snow is gone, the waters have receded, and the trails are completely dried out. All basins and cirques, no matter how remote, are, for this brief time, fully accessible to foot travel. The flowers of the highest tundra (above 12,000 feet) begin to succumb to frost in the final weeks of August.

SEPTEMBER

For many people, September is the only time for the Indian Peaks. The aspens are turning gold, and the high tundra is deepening with scarlets and maroons and oranges. Everywhere the green of summer is fading. Ducks and geese stop overnight on lakes and ponds as they migrate south. Flocks of migrating songbirds are frequently observed. The insects are gone, as are the summer crowds. The elk are bugling in the deep woods, and the bowhunters are quietly about pursuing their craft. With streams running extremely low, the fly fisherman finally has his day, finding the elusive trout of the remote pools. The tundra is normally very dry in September, and many of the smaller, seasonal streams have completely dried up. The air freezes most every night, and snow may briefly appear in the high peaks, only to evaporate within a few hours. The Earth begins to lose its warmth. Many popular places crowded in the summer are deserted now, especially on the Western Slope, and you can have parts of the Indian Peaks all to yourself.

WINTER

What can you say? The winter in the Indian Peaks is similar to that found around the arctic circle. Winds are regular and severe, blizzards and whiteouts are frequent, and temperatures often drop far below zero. At certain times, the northern lights can be seen. Snow caves or expedition tents are required to safely pass the night. Still, nearly every day, skiers and snowshoers can be seen in popular touring areas braving the bitter cold for the challenge of vigorous outdoor exercise and the supreme beauty of the snowbound wilderness.

A WILDERNESS ETHIC

The chief objective of any wilderness ethic is, of course, minimum impact. Travelers should strive to leave the ecosystem exactly as they find it—an undisturbed natural laboratory where the subtle adaptive and creative forces of nature can work freely and without interference by man. With this in mind, a few simple principles should be remembered: (1) Scrupulously obey all official regulations pertaining to travel in the Indian Peaks, particularly with respect to camping and campfires. Also observe fish and game regulations. (2) Avoid shortcuts and endeavor to remain on established trails. (3) Camp on nonvegetated soil when possible to avoid killing fragile plants. (4) Be considerate of others when camping and remain as quiet and out of the way as possible. (5) Don't build any permanent structures, like cairns, or scar trees with a knife or axe. (6) Pack out everything you pack in. (7) Use a gas stove when possible. (8) In areas where it is permitted, keep your campfire small and restore the area to its natural appearance before you leave. (9) Don't use soap in or around lakes or streams. (10) Dispose of wastes in holes six inches deep and at least 200 feet from moving or standing water. (11) Never pick wild flowers or disturb wildlife. (12) Leave your pets at home. No one appreciates a loud dog, least of all the wild creatures who call this place home. (13) When approaching horses on the trail, give them the right-of-way. Any sudden movement can alarm a horse and cause a serious accident for the rider.

A NOTE ON TECHNICAL CLIMBING

Most of the good technical climbing in this area is outside of the Indian Peaks in Eldorado Canyon, Boulder Canyon, and Rocky Mountain National Park. The prevalent rock of the summits and lower ridges is Idaho Springs schist and gneiss, as well as granite, while that of the lower canyons and hogbacks is fountain sandstone. Whole books have been devoted to ascents of Long's Peak, which has everything from easy digressions from the main foot trail to the world-famous "Diamond" which tops the "E" face. Also notable in the park are Sharkstooth, the cliffs of Hallet, and lower granites such as the Needle and Thumb and Teddy's Teeth. Lone Eagle Peak, in the Upper Cascade Creed drainage, probably offers the best climbing in the Indian Peaks. The rock is generally sound and provides some fine technical climbs, but it has also claimed several fatalities. There are also some less frequently visited peaks in the wilderness with some truly horrendous walls. Any technical climbing should be attempted only by seasoned mountaineers, or under the close direction of a professional guide.

CAMERAS IN THE HIGH COUNTRY

Whether you travel on foot, by horse, or on skis, you will probably take a camera. The scenery, particularly on the Eastern Slope, is spectacular. Basic equipment should include a 35 mm camera, at least one roll of thirty-six exposures for each day on the trail, and lens cleaner. Beyond that, most people carry one or more of the following: a wide-angle lens, a 90 mm or 135 mm telephoto lens (and a tripod if you pack a 200 mm lens), and a macro lens for closeups of wild flowers.

In the high country there are extremely sharp lighting contrasts. Use a light meter, preferably one that measures spot as well as average readings. Snow and ice will fool your meter. Open the diaphragm two stops more than the meter indicates in order to compensate for glare. Above timberline there is so much sky that the extra light will also confuse your meter. For more realistic readings, aim the meter more toward the ground than you normally would. If your camera has a lens meter, it lacks the accuracy of a separate meter. With the attached meter, you are more likely to get the photo you want if you bracket the shot with several exposures.

A medium-speed color film should handle most situations. It gives you more flexibility in dark forests and handles all lighting with more color warmth than high-speed film. Use a medium yellow filter if you're shooting black and white.

EQUIPMENT IN PRIMITIVE AREAS

The following is a fairly complete list of recommended equipment to take with you into the Indian Peaks:

I. Essential Equipment

Backpacking tent
Comfortable hiking boots (To avoid blisters, use talcum or foot powder and wear light nylon socks beneath your heavier socks.)
Appropriate clothing (Carry sufficient clothing for the length and season of your trip. Dress in layers, as temperatures fluctuate suddenly throughout the year.)
Lightweight aluminum frame backpack and baffled goose or duck down sleeping bag
Gas stove (and extra fuel canister)
Sierra cup and eating bowl
Aluminum pan and handle
Aluminum pot and eating utensils
Two 1-quart plastic water containers
Halozone tablets
Brillo pad and biodegradable soap
Waterproof matches and candles
Flashlight and extra batteries
Poncho
20 to 30 feet of 1/8" nylon cord
Pocket knife

Foam sleeping pad
First aid kit (To include sunburn lotion and/or protective cream,
   Chapstick, moleskin, aspirin, bandaids, roll gauze, adhesive
   tape, and ace bandage)
Map (standard 7 1/2' USGA topographic maps are the best)
Toothbrush and toothpaste
Toilet paper
G.I. can opener
Sunglasses and brimmed hat
Compass, mirror, and whistle
Emergency repair kit (needle, thread, wire, cord, screws)
Small towel
Comb

II. Optional Equipment

Camera and film
Fishing gear and license
Binoculars
Magnifying glass
Notebook and pencil, book to read
Vitamin tablets
Day pack (for side excursions)
Face mask or balaclava (winter travel)
Ice axe, crampons, climbing rope (winter travel)

III. Food Ideas (1 pound to 1.5 pound/day)

Standard freeze-dried foods
High-energy foods (e.g., hard candy, nuts, dried fruit)
Instant soup, coffee, cocoa, hot chocolate, orange and tomato
   juice
Pilot biscuits
Rice
Ramon noodles
Eggs (in hard plastic containers)
Spaghetti noodles (and powdered sauce)
Potato flakes
Canned tuna
Powdered milk
Hard sausage or pepperoni
Cheese and crackers
Jerky
Tortillas

Peanut butter and honey
Teabags and sugar
Oatmeal (with brown sugar and powdered milk)
Salt and pepper
Fresh trout
Fresh berries (blueberries, huckleberries, raspberries, serviceberries, thimbleberries)

IMPORTANT ADDRESSES AND INFORMATION

USFS
Boulder District Office
2995 Baseline - Room 16
Boulder, Colorado 80303
(303) 444-6003; Mon - Fri 8 - 5

USFS
Estes Park Office
161 Second Street
Estes Park, Colorado 80517
(303) 586-3440; Mon - Fri 8 - 5
(Open 6/1 - 9/1 only)

USFS
Sulphur District Office
100 U.S. Highway 34
Granby, Colorado 80446
(303) 887-3331
Mon - Thur 8 - 5
Fri 8 - 8

USFS
Supervisor's Office
240 West Prospect
Ft. Collins, Colorado 80526
(303) 221-4390
Mon - Fri 8 - 5

Topographic maps should always be used for wilderness travel. The following maps cover the Indian Peaks area: Monarch Lake, Isolation Peak, Ward, Shadow Mountain, Allenspark, East Portal, and Nederland. They may be purchased directly from local sporting goods and outdoor stores or from the U.S. Geological Survey, at the following address:

USGS Map Store
Box 25286
Denver Federal Center
Denver, Colorado 80225

NEW RULES AND REGULATIONS

Effective June 1, 1984, an entirely new permit system is being implemented in the Indian Peaks. The system was developed for the following reasons: (1) To limit use through the establishment of a quota. Heavy use has resulted in unacceptable damage to the subalpine forests and to the alpine landscape itself. (2) To provide visitors with information on regulations, ethics, and current conditions, and (3) To collect data on use so that the government can better manage the wilderness and improve the backcountry experience.

As a result of this decision, the government had divided the Indian Peaks into fifteen travel zones, each zone with a separate daily quota. Eventually, some of the more popular alpine lakes may have designated campsites, as is the case in Rocky Mountain National Park just to the north. Hikers should contact the Forest Service for more information.

HAZARDS IN THE WILDERNESS

The Indian Peaks is a region of unusually hazardous weather and climbing conditions throughout the year. Some of the strongest winds ever recorded have been measured on Niwot Ridge, with gusts sometimes exceeding 160 miles per hour. Gusts of eighty miles per hour are not uncommon, particularly in the winter and spring, when fronts push through quickly. These winds can result

WIND SPEED	COOLING POWER OF WIND EXPRESSED AS EQUIVALENT CHILL TEMPERATURE									
MPH	TEMPERATURE (°F)									
CALM	40	30	20	10	5	0	-10	-20	-30	-40	-50	-60
	EQUIVALENT CHILL TEMPERATURE									
5	35	25	15	5	0	-5	-15	-25	-35	-45	-55	-70
10	30	15	5	-10	-15	-20	-35	-45	-60	-70	-80	-95
15	25	10	-5	-20	-25	-30	-45	-60	-70	-85	-100	-110
20	20	5	-10	-25	-30	-35	-50	-65	-80	-95	-110	-120
25	15	0	-15	-30	-35	-45	-60	-75	-90	-105	-120	-135
30	10	0	-20	-30	-40	-50	-65	-80	-95	-110	-125	-140
35	10	-5	-20	-35	-40	-50	-65	-80	-100	-115	-130	-145
40	10	-5	-20	-35	-45	-55	-70	-85	-100	-115	-130	-150
	LITTLE DANGER			INCREASING DANGER (Flesh may freeze within 1 min.)				GREAT DANGER (Flesh may freeze within 30 seconds)			

Frostbite or hypothermia are the common dangers resulting from wind, temperature and moisture.

in deadly conditions in which exposed flesh freezes instantly. The rugged and remote character of the terrain also presents a danger to the backcountry traveler, particularly one who is inexperienced. The following is a list of the more common hazards in the wilderness, and how to avoid them.

FORDING STREAMS

Every year one or two people drown in Front Range streams during the spring runoff (usually from late May to early July). Most of these fatalities can be attributed to simple lack of experience or poor judgment. Frequently, the victims are from the East and are unaware of the danger of mountain water—of its surprising depth and the terrific strength of its current. Do not attempt to cross any moving water that appears even remotely hazardous. Many crossings are impossible until late in the summer.

LIGHTNING

Severe thunderstorms, sometimes accompanied by sleet, hail, and gale-force winds, are common in the summer. Temperatures can drop fifty degrees in minutes. Whiteout conditions can occur. Lightning is the chief hazard of these storms. It prefers to strike, as a downstroke or an upstroke, the highest point or peak, the edge of cliffs, isolated trees, or the largest object in an open area. Storms rarely develop without giving the wilderness traveler ample warning. If, however, you are caught in a bad situation, authorities recommend that you crouch down (not lie down) on some kind of dry, insulating material, such as a sleeping bag. Remove all metallic objects, as they will cause serious burns if you are electrocuted. Avoid cliff faces, as the exploding bolt will radiate out from the rock. Also avoid shallow caves. If a companion is struck by lightning, immediately begin closed heart massage, mouth-to-mouth resuscitation, and, if the victim is revived, treat for shock.

ROCK CLIMBING AND SNOWFIELDS

Once again, every year one or two people die as a result of falls in the Front Range. Typically, they climb up a steep slab surface and then discover that they cannot retrace their path back down. Suddenly aware of their dangerous situation, they panic and fall. Serious fractures, concussions, lacerations, bruises, and even paralysis can

Almost thirty switchbacks lead up this steep slope on the west side of Pawnee Pass. Hikers should always be careful in such rocky and remote country. Courtesy Linda Elinoff.

result. Loose rock, as is found in talus slides everywhere, is more of a hazard than most people think. Finally, the innocent sport of sliding down the permanent and lingering snowfields that abound in the Indian Peaks can result in serious injury when the participants find they cannot stop, and strike boulders and rocks at high speed.

AVALANCHES

The chief hazard in the winter, next to exposure, is that of the avalanche. Many people needlessly die in avalanches every year in the backcountry. In most cases these accidents could have been avoided. Even small avalanches pack extremely destructive power, moving tons of snow at speeds sometimes in excess of 100 miles per hour. There are two forms of avalanche: the loose snow and the slab avalanche. Loose snow moves as a formless mass with little internal cohesion, while slab avalanches consist of an entire angular block or chunk of snow. Practically all fatalities are caused by the latter, whose initial movement is caused by the victims themselves.

Several simple precautions can help avoid this hazard. First, avoid old avalanche paths, steep, open gullies, and long slopes. Beware when snow begins to roll spontaneously down the slope or if you observe an avalanche anywhere in the vicinity. If the snow sounds hollow, particularly on a leeward slope, or if the snow cracks and continues to run, immediately leave the area. Islands of safety include dense timber, ridges, or rocky outcrops. If you must cross a dangerous slope, stay high and near the top. Let only one person cross at a time. Carry and use an avalanche cord, and carry a sectional probe. Avalanche transcievers (beacons) are also an effective safety device. Beware of sustained wind conditions, freshly falling snow, or fluctuating temperatures, all of which contribute to avalanche danger.

If your group has the misfortune of being caught in an

avalanche, and you survive, mark the place where you last saw the victim, and search for him or her below the last seen point, probing deeply and regularly with a ski pole. Remember—you are the victim's only chance for survival. Do not leave unless help is only a few minutes away. After one hour, the victim has less than a fifty percent chance of surviving. If there are others, send only one person for help while the others continue to search. If you find the victim, treat for suffocation.

If you are caught in an avalanche, make swimming motions, as you would in heavy surf, trying to stay on top and to work your way to the side of the avalanche. The avalanche, which shares the characteristics of a liquid, will try to bury you underneath it, just as a crashing wave drags you to the bottom of the beach. Before coming to a stop, place your hands in front of your face, and try to make an air space in the snow as you are coming to a stop.

HYPOTHERMIA

A combination of exertion and rain, snow, sleet, or wind can cause hypothermia, as can crossing or falling into a stream. Hypothermia occurs when the victim's body temperature drops too low to sustain life. Symptoms include uncontrollable shivering, cold extremities, and a confused and eventually listless state of mind. To treat the victim, immediately wrap in dry, warm clothing (or a sleeping bag) and administer warm fluids. In extreme cases, it might be necessary for another person to enter the sleeping bag in order to transfer body heat.

HYPOXIA

Also known as altitude or mountain sickness, hypoxia

afflicts some people at elevations above 8,000 feet. It has a variety of symptoms, some as mild as a headache, nausea, a feeling of weakness or indolence, and a poor appetite. More serious symptoms include dizziness, disorientation, impaired judgment, retinal bleeding, and, in severe cases, pulmonary edema. The victim should descend to a lower altitude and seek medical assistance.

HEART FAILURE

At the first sign of pain, numbness, or tingling in the chest, neck, or arms, or extreme dizziness or faintheadedness, immediately descend to a lower altitude and seek medical assistance.

SUNBURN

The alpine sun can quickly cause severe burns of exposed skin. Chronic exposure at this elevation destroys the body's ability to fight back against cancer cells in the epidermis, resulting in skin cancer, which can be fatal when it spreads to other organs and systems of the body. Colorado has the highest rate of skin cancer in the nation as a result of its high altitude.

GIARDIA LAMBLIA

Giardia is an intestinal parasite found in animal feces, particularly beaver, which pollutes mountain streams and causes serious gastrointestinal symptoms referred to medically as giardiasis. Nicknamed "beaver fever" in the mountains, it is even more debilitating than "turista," which afflicts travelers south of the border. Symptoms include painful intestinal cramps, gas, and severe diarrhea. Dehydration, dizziness, disorientation, and extreme fatigue can result. Medical attention should be sought. It is important to keep fluid and salt levels up. To avoid dysentery, boil or treat all water.

BEING LOST

If you find yourself lost, don't panic. Relax, sit down, study your maps and surroundings, and listen for sounds that may give you a clue to your whereabouts. Remember that the sun and moon rise and set from east to west. All major drainages soon lead to civilization. If you must spend the night unplanned in the mountains, and are sufficiently prepared (you should always have emergency gear in a day pack for even short hikes), it should be no problem. If you have told people of your trip's itinerary and duration, help should soon arrive. Both Boulder and Grand counties have excellent search and rescue teams. Probably the most important thing in any crisis is to have a sense of humor and a little common sense.

BEARS

A few simple rules should prevent any mishaps with the local bears. Never approach an unattended cub. The sow is always nearby. Never leave food unattended around camp. Always hoist food supplies into a tree some distance from your sleeping area at night. Never camp in an area where you observe fresh bear droppings, diggings, or tracks. If you find yourself face to face with a bear, don't run. A sign of fear, this will simply trigger the animal's instinct to attack. He can run as fast as a horse. You can't. Throw your pack down to distract and delay him. Walk calmly to the nearest tree and climb it as high as you can. Even if you have never climbed a tree before, you should have no problem now. Hopefully the bear will then go for your pack. After all, the bear is hungry. Like Falstaff, bears are always hungry. If you are attacked, play dead. Lie down on the ground and curl up with your knees tucked against your chest. Keep your hands behind your head and neck. Sometimes it works. The bear will simply sniff around, bite you a few times, and then cover you up with dirt. Finally, always make a little noise that is unmistakably human as you move through heavy brush or timber.

HUNTING AND FISHING

Current regulations for hunting and fishing can be acquired from the Colorado Division of Wildlife, 6060 Broadway, Denver, Colorado 80216 (303) 297-1192. Big game species commonly hunted in the wilderness and surrounding national forests include mule deer, elk, and black bear. Most hunters agree that the Indian Peaks offer poor hunting for big game and prefer areas on the Western Slope where the game exists in greater numbers, people are fewer, and the terrain is not as rugged.

Fishing for trout in the Indian Peaks runs from poor to excellent, depending on the water. Recent transplants into Brainard and Long lakes on the Eastern Slope should improve fishing there, as well as regulations on the exclusive use of flies and lures. Rainbow Lakes is traditionally a well-stocked area in which to fish. On the Western Slope, both the Buchanan and Arapaho creek drainages offer good fishing for brook trout. Some of the more remote lakes and streams can be good later in the summer. As with hunting, better fishing is found elsewhere, the quality of which is usually a direct function of the remoteness of the water.

PART III
Wilderness Trails

Here we had plenty of wood, water, meat and dry grass to sleep on, and taking everything into consideration we thought ourselves comfortably situated. Comfortably I say for mountaineers. . .experience is the best Teacher, hunger good sauce and I really think to be acquainted with misery contributes to the enjoyment of happiness, and to know ones self greatly facilitates Knowledge of Mankind. One thing I often console myself with, and that is the earth will lie as hard upon the Monarch as it will on a Hunter, and I have no assurance that it will lie upon me at all; my bones may in a few years or perhaps days be bleaching on the plains in these regions, like many of my occupation without a friend to turn even a turf upon them after a hungry wolf has finished his feast."

—Osborne Russell
Journal of a Trapper
Lincoln, Nebraska
University of Nebraska Press, 1955

TRAILS WEST
OF THE DIVIDE

Three major trail systems Arapaho, Cascade, and Buchanan Creek—originate here at peaceful Monarch Lake on the Western Slope. Courtesy Charles W. Murray, Jr.

Trails on the Western Slope of the Indian Peaks Wilderness are more centrally located and easily reached than those on the Eastern Slope and are for the most part less crowded. All but the Corona, Caribou Pass, and Columbine Lake trailheads are found in the immediate vicinity of Monarch Lake, which is ten miles east of U.S. Highway 34 on the unpaved road (County Road 6) that follows the southern shores of Lake Granby. The turnoff is distinctly visible on the right of the highway and difficult to miss.

The Corona, Caribou Pass, and Columbine Lake trailheads are reached by turning off U.S. Highway 34 just before the mountain village of Tabernash on Forest Service Route 129, which follows Meadow Creek nine miles to Meadow Creek Reservoir. Connections can be made there on the High Lonesome Trail back up north to Monarch Lake. Wildlife is more often seen on the Western Slope than on the Eastern Slope, vegetation tends to be more lush as westerly storm systems stall against the Continental Divide, and there are fewer people, making for a more enjoyable wilderness experience. It is well worth the two hour drive from Denver.

1. ARAPAHO PASS TRAIL

Trailhead elevation: 8,360 feet
Total vertical ascent: 3,546 feet
Trail ending: 11,906 feet
Length: 9.3 miles (15 kilometers)
Recommended season: July 1 to September 15
Use: Moderate
Difficulty: Moderate
USGS maps: Monarch Lake
Trail profile:

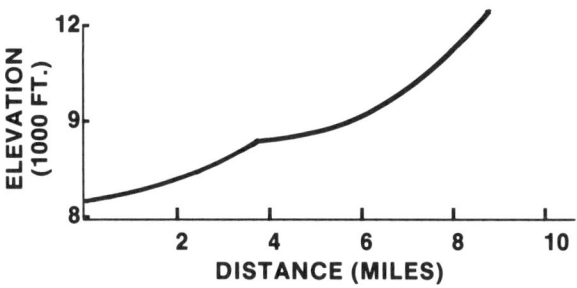

Access:

There are three means of access to the Arapaho Pass Trail. (1) From Monarch Lake, follow the Southside Trail 1.5 miles around Monarch Lake to the Arapaho Pass Trail sign on the right. (2) Via the Caribou Pass Trail from Meadow Creek Reservoir (4.4 miles), the trail junction being Arapaho Pass. (3) Take Highway 119 to the Eldora Road south of Nederland. Follow this road past the turnoff to the winter ski area and through the town, to where it becomes an unimproved dirt road. Take the right fork 1 mile out of Eldora, and continue 3.5 miles up to Buckingham Campground and the Fourth of July Trailhead.

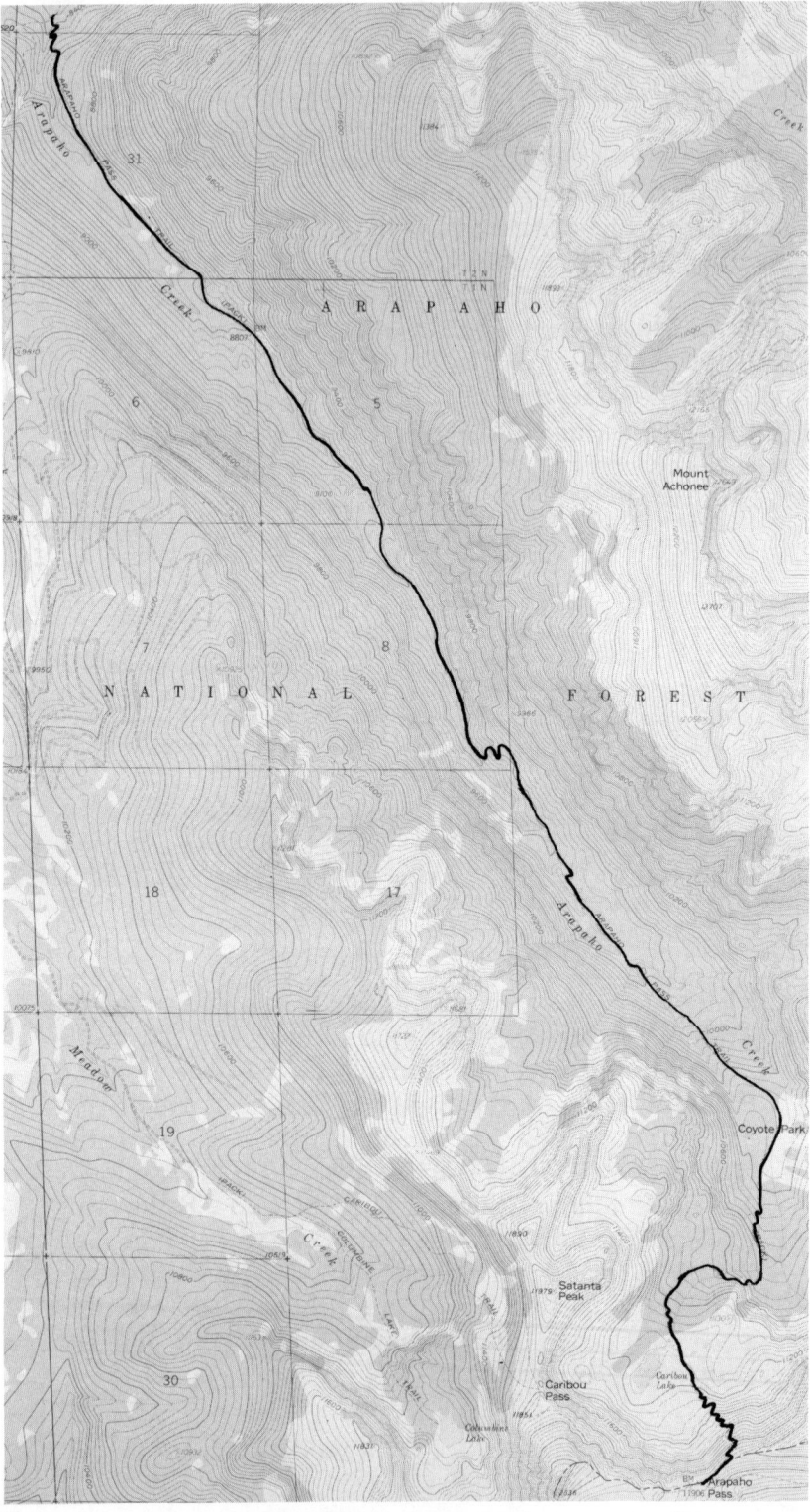

Starting from Monarch Lake, the Arapaho Pass Trail begins with a series of switchbacks that climb through a steep hillside forest of lodgepole pine. The trail then levels out, passes several rock slides, and traverses a slope high above Arapaho Creek, which can be heard rushing in the canyon below. The trail follows the creek on the east side of the drainage through thick forests of Englemann spruce, lodgepole pine, and subalpine fir that almost completely shade the trail, even at midday.

At several junctures, small side trails, sometimes covered with fresh deer, elk, coyote, and bear tracks, lead down to Arapaho Creek. Arapaho Creek has an abundance of deep pools and miniature cascades formed by the many log jams, fallen trees, and large boulders. The playful and cheerful water ouzel is often observed in and around the water. Fishing for brook trout can be good in many of the pools after the runoff.

Chair Rock, on upper Arapaho Creek, was formed naturally by frost action on the cliffs above. Courtesy Charles W. Murray, Jr.

Arapaho Creek, in late summer, just below Coyote Park. Courtesy Charles W. Murray, Jr.

In several places along the trail where sunlight manages to penetrate the gloom of the thick forest, wild flowers and berries abound. These include blueberries, strawberries, raspberries, monkshood, bluebells, and the penstemon bloom. Old man's beard, a green-grey colored lichen somewhat similar in appearance to the Spanish moss that festoons the live oaks of the Deep South, hangs from many of the evergreens, giving the forest an eerie quality, like those mythical mid-summer woods of Shakespeare's Oberon and Titania. Porcupines abound in these woods and are often seen.

About 3.2 miles up the trail are the remains of a 1974 mud slide in which a twenty-foot wide slide of mud, rocks, and trees crossed the trail to the stream. Just beyond the slide, the trail ascends a steep incline in four long switchbacks. Four and three-quarters miles up the trail is a

An abandoned cabin near Caribou Lake (11,147 feet) at the headwaters of Arapaho Creek. Mount Achonee (12,649 feet) dominates in the background. Courtesy Charles W. Murray, Jr.

perfect resting spot in the form of Chair Rock, a rock that was frost heaved from the cliffs above and has the striking appearance of a natural chair. It is a good place to take a breather, get some refreshments, and take a photograph of your companion sitting in the chair.

Past Chair Rock, the trail enters an even denser spruce jungle and eventually crosses a log bridge over Arapaho Creek, 5.2 miles from the beginning of the trail. From that point, the trail steepens as it passes a large avalanche slide area and crosses several small brooks draining the Wheeler Basin area (a favorite summer range for the reclusive bull elk and buck deer).

The trail then enters Coyote Park, a large subalpine meadow of deep grass and a variety of native wild flowers, including yellow snowlillies, Indian paintbrush, and American bistort, as they are found in season. Deer and elk and occasionally coyotes are seen here near dusk and dawn and are best photographed with a telephoto lens. Lighting conditions at those times can be tricky, and special attention should be given to settings and film.

The trail soon reenters the forest for about another mile before reaching the shores of Caribou Lake, 11,851 feet, nestled in a cirque between Arapaho Pass and Caribou Pass. The view includes the jagged Apache and Navajo peaks to the northeast and the open alpine meadows to the northwest. The trail continues above the eastern shore of the lake in a steep series of tight switchbacks to Arapaho Pass and the Continental Divide. Several rare wildflowers, including the dwarf fireweed, are found here and could be easily killed by careless shortcuts over the tundra between switchbacks. The pass is a good location to observe Satanta (11,979 feet), South Arapaho (13,397 feet), and North Arapaho Peaks (13,501 feet), and the North Fork Creek drainage on the east side of the divide.

2. CARIBOU PASS TRAIL

Trailhead elevation: 10,050 feet
Total vertical ascent: 1,740 feet
Trail ending: 11,790 feet
Length: 3.2 miles (5.1 kilometers)
Recommended season: July 1 to September 15
Use: Medium
Difficulty: Difficult
USGS maps: Monarch Lake
Trail profile:

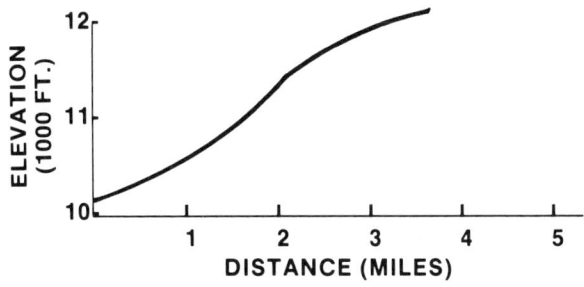

Access:

Turn right or northeast on forest service road number 129 just before Tabernash on U.S. 40. Drive approximately ten miles northwest on this road. The Caribou Pass Trailhead is located on the road above Meadow Creek Reservoir at the parking area to Junco Lake.

The Caribou Pass Trail is short and intense, leading to a very fine overlook of the Indian Peaks. One juncture of the trail leads to beautiful Columbine Lake, located at 11,200

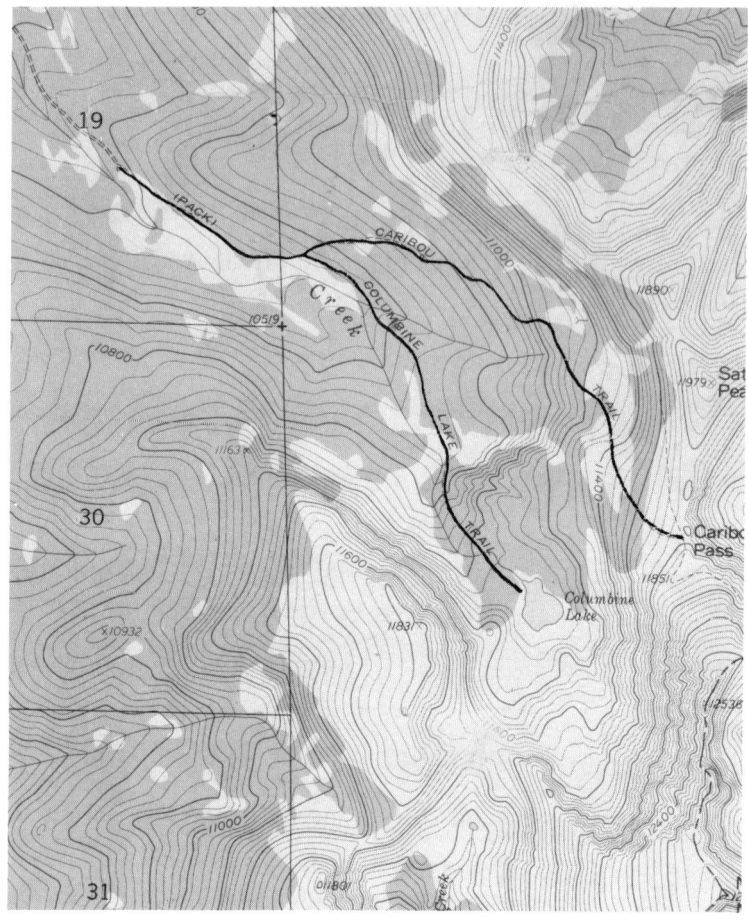

feet at the base of Mount Neva (12,814 feet). This site is seldom visited by wilderness travelers. Although not one of the more important trails of the wilderness area, the Pass Trail is not without its virtues.

Just past Junco Lake (10,039 feet), the Caribou Pass Trail follows Meadow Creek through a subalpine forest past two disintegrating old log cabins, perhaps used by ranchers or miners at the turn of the century or earlier. The trail is quite slippery in places and, where it has fallen away at two

From Caribou Pass, looking east, one can see the many switchbacks of Arapaho Pass climbing above Caribou Lake. Courtesy U.S. Forest Service.

points, it may in fact be unsuitable for horses. At mile 1.7, the trail splits, the left fork continuing another 1.5 miles to the saddle of the pass, and the right fork crossing over the north fork of Meadow Creek south toward Columbine Lake.

Following the juncture, the Columbine Lake Trail gradually ascends to the edge of the spruce and fir forest and then increases in steepness. Two small, level meadows are passed before the trail crosses the creek. Shortly thereafter, the trail reaches the level of Columbine Lake and passes through some krummholz just at tree line, 3.0 miles from the trailhead. Mount Neva (12,814 feet) is almost wholly obscured by rugged rock, but it can be climbed from Columbine Lake by circling to the right around the western shore and ascending a trail to a pass in the ridge just south of the lake. The climb from the pass to the summit, along the ridge, is fairly self-evident.

The Caribou Pass Trail continues beyond the juncture with the Columbine Lake trail through thick subalpine forest and meadows, crossing several small sidestreams, bogs, and abandoned mines. The ascent toward the pass is not difficult for anyone in good shape, even with a backpack. There are far more demanding passes (such as Pawnee Pass) in the Indian Peaks. If you have come from a lower elevation and are not physically acclimated yet, it is a good idea to make frequent stops and let your heart and lungs adjust to the rigors of the altitude, which has far less oxygen than other parts of the country.

The view from Caribou Pass to the east is excellent including Apache Peak (13,441 feet), Navajo Peak (13,409 feet), and Caribou Lake. A short .5 mile to the north brings you to the summit of Satanta Peak (11,979 feet). Another .5 mile to the south finds you on the shores of the highest lake in the Indian Peaks—Lake Dorothy (12,051 feet).

3. CORONA TRAIL

Trailhead elevation: 11,670 feet (from Rollins Pass)
Total vertical ascent: 2,010 feet
Trail ending: 9,660 feet
Length: 6 miles (9.6 kilometers)
Recommended season: July 1 to September 15
Use: Light
Difficulty: Moderate to Difficult
USGS maps: East Portal
Trail profile:

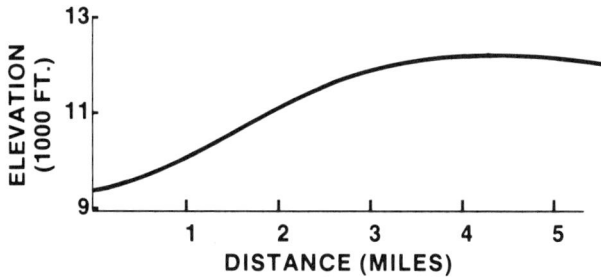

Access:

There are three means of access to the Corona Trail. (1) From Rollins Pass, follow the old jeep road to the northwest until you reach the wilderness boundary sign. (2) Begin in Devil's Thumb Park at the junction of the High Lonesome and Corona trails. (3) From Devil's Thumb Pass above Devil's Thumb Lake on the Eastern Slope, which meets the Corona Trail at the Pass.

This trail covers six miles from Devil's Thumb Park to Rollins Pass, with Devil's Thumb Pass located approximately midway. Many climbing enthusiasts use this

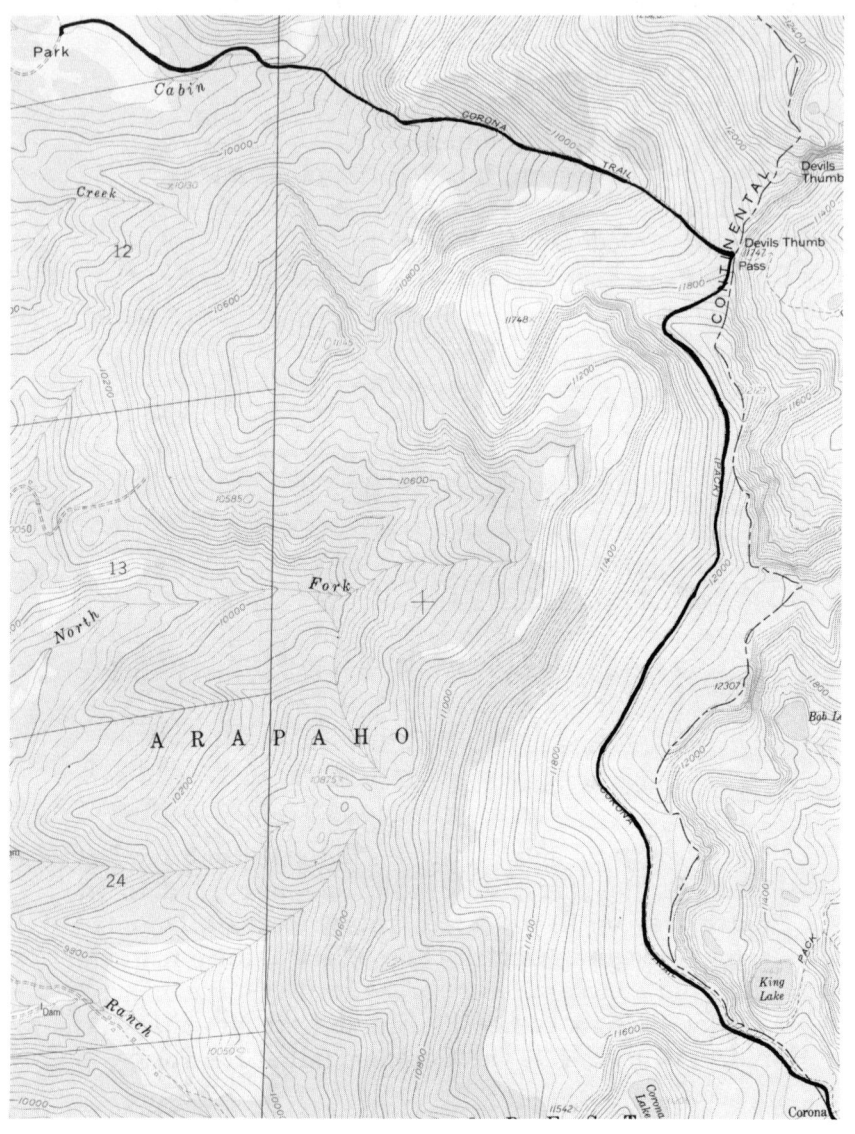

There are very few chances to find water on the Corona Trail, which is entirely above timberline. Courtesy U.S. Forest Service.

trail to reach the popular Devil's Thumb, which protrudes from the Divide near the pass which is named for it. The entire hike from Devil's Thumb Pass to Rollins Pass is above timberline and can be the site of sudden and dangerous thunderstorms and snowstorms. Little if any water is available on the tundra, so a water bottle is a necessity.

From Devil's Thumb Park, the trail meanders through the valley, frequently crossing Cabin Creek before it begins its steep ascent through a subalpine forest to Devil's Thumb Pass. As you approach the saddle or pass from below, the Devil's Thumb soon comes prominently into view. The thumb itself can be reached by hiking northward along the Divide about .25 mile from the pass. There are many ptarmigan in this area.

The actual Corona Trail turns sharply to the south from the pass, while another trail, the Devil's Thumb Trail, runs down the steep eastern slopes of the Divide toward Devil's Thumb and Jasper Lakes. The remaining 3.5 miles to Rollins Pass is an easy hike if the weather is good.

Camping on the tundra is damaging to the vegetation and dangerous for campers in the event of a sudden electrical storm. The only good camping is in Devil's Thumb Park or on the Eastern Slope around the upper lakes of the Boulder Creek drainage. The view to the west over Middle Park to the drainage of the Colorado River and the southern summits of North Park, and to the east of the familiar Front Range country is spectacular. Just before reaching Rollins Pass, approximately .3 mile, a small trail heads down toward King Lake and Bob and Betty lakes, which are visible below.

4. HIGH LONESOME TRAIL

Trailhead elevation: 8,360 feet
Total vertical ascent: 1,600 feet
Trail ending: 9,960 feet
Length: 4.1 miles (6.6 kilometers)
Recommended season: June 20 to September 30
Use: Light
Difficulty: Moderate
USGS maps: Monarch Lake
Trail profile:

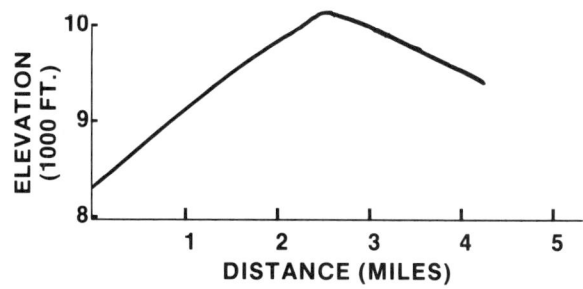

Access:

There are two means of access to the High Lonesome Trail. (1) From Devil's Thumb Park, just past the juncture of Devil's Thumb Pass or Corona Trail and over Cabin Creek. (2) 1.5 miles from the parking lot at Monarch Lake, where the High Lonesome Trail branches off to the right (west) from the Arapaho Pass Trail.

The High Lonesome Trail is named for the High Lonesome Mine, which is now abandoned, and connects Monarch Lake on the north with Meadow Creek Reservoir

67

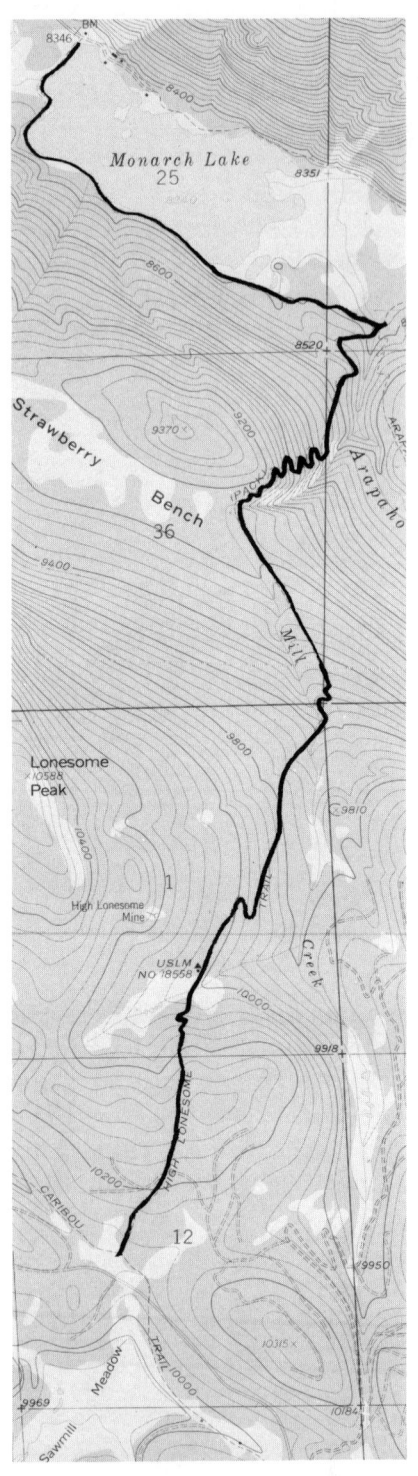

in the south. It is a popular trail with deer and elk hunters in the fall, but it is seldom used in the summer months, as it does not lead into the high country and boasts no spectacular scenery. Not far from the trail junction are the ruins of a pre-1900 cabin and another 2.5 miles further on is the abandoned mine. The trail ends not far from Meadow Creek Reservoir.

After crossing Arapaho Creek, the High Lonesome Trail steadily ascends the eastern portion of the ridge just to the south of Monarch Lake. This is a popular winter denning area for bears, who also enjoy ranging through the swampy areas of Strawberry Bench during the summer. Their fresh tracks and droppings are commonly found on the High Lonesome Trail.

After .5 mile, the trail twists through some steep switchbacks in the lodgepole pine before it crosses Mill Creek for the first time. The trail becomes more gentle beyond the crossing and then crosses over Mill Creek for the second and last time in what is now a very dense stand of spruce and fir. Just over the 10,000-foot level, and before a series of beaver ponds on a western tributary to Mill Creek, is a government land marker. The trail then ascends over a small hill before turning down toward Meadow Creek Reservoir.

Another segment of the High Lonesome Trail, which runs entirely outside the wilderness, connects Meadow Creek Reservoir with Devil's Thumb Park.

5. CASCADE CREEK TRAIL

Trailhead elevation: 8,346 feet
Total vertical ascent: 4,195 feet
Trail ending (Pawnee Pass): 12,541 feet
Length: 10.5 miles (16.9 kilometers)
Recommended season: July 1 to September 15
Use: Heavy
Difficulty: Very difficult
USGS maps: Monarch Lake
Trail profile:

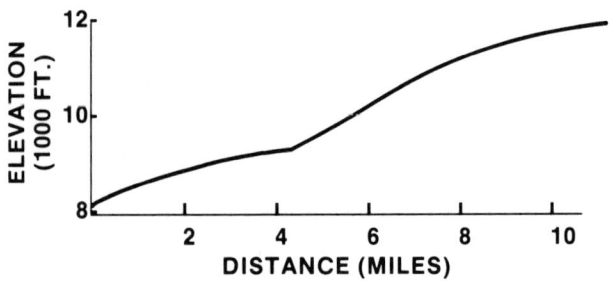

Access:

Take Highway 34 to County Road 6, 5.4 miles north of Granby and 8.9 miles south of Grand Lake. Turn right or east at the juncture. Follow this unpaved road 9.4 miles along Granby Reservoir to Monarch Lake, where parking is available. The Cascade Creek Trail follows the north shore of Monarch Lake.

One of the major east-west trails in the Indian Peaks, the Cascade Creek Trail is also the most popular trail on the Western Slope, particularly on weekends and holidays in

Cascades, for which Cascade Creek is named, are found in abundance throughout its length. Courtesy Charles W. Murray, Jr.

the summer. Numerous campsites are available along the entirety of its length, scenery is spectacular in the upper reaches of the various drainages served by the trail, and fishing is generally good in all of the water, including the several lakes. Horses, which can be rented at the Arapahoe Ranch just below Monarch Lake, are not permitted past Cascade Falls, approximately four miles up Cascade Creek. Waterfalls and cascades abound in this area, as well as meadows full of larkspur, columbine, Indian paintbrush, and lupine. In some years of heavy rainfall, these wild flowers can grow five or six feet tall and loom densely on either side of the trail as it passes through the upper meadows, creating an almost *Garden of Eden* quality about the place.

The Cascade Creek Trail follows the north shore of

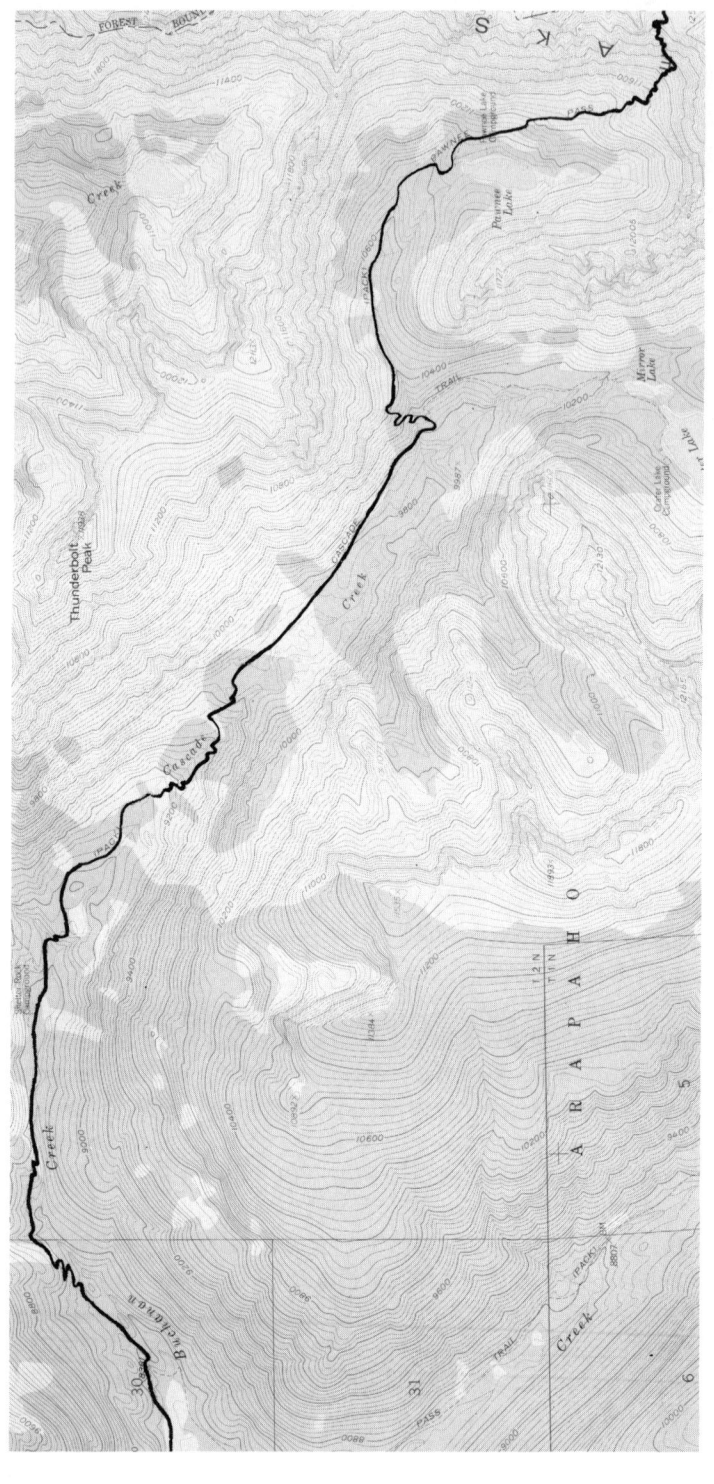

The subalpine beaver meadows above Cascade Falls. Courtesy Charles W. Murray, Jr.

Monarch Lake for 1.5 miles before reaching the Arapaho-Cascade Trail junction. The fork to the right shortly crosses a bridge and leads to the Arapaho Creek drainage. The Cascade Trail continues on to the left and soon begins a moderate climb through a lodgepole pine forest. Shelter Rock (8,800 feet), an enormous boulder left by the glaciers, is reached after a 3.25-mile hike that includes two switchback areas and a bridge across the stream that drains Hells Canyon. From Shelter Rock, Buchanan Creek can be heard rushing by not far south of the Cascade Creek Trail. It is illegal to camp at Shelter Rock because it is located within 100 feet of the trail.

The Cascade Trail then crosses Buchanan Creek and once again joins Cascade Creek. It is soon evident, from the many cascades, how Cascade Creek got its name. Many

Pawnee Lake (10,804 feet), as seen from the far western side of Pawnee Pass. Middle Park can be discerned in the far background. Courtesy Linda Elinoff.

pleasant hours can be spent next to these lovely cascades, engaging in leisurely conversation with companions, or simply listening to the water in solitude.

The trail soon climbs a steep switchback along the edge of one of the many canyons cut by Cascade Creek. After 4.3 miles, the trail crosses the creek and some beaver ponds before heading up another series of switchbacks, these shorter than the first. Halfway up these switchbacks are the spectacular Cascade Falls, a good place to take photographs.

Above Cascade Falls, the trail once more crosses the creek and begins a rather brisk climb to the next glacier-cut shelf. Five miles up the trail, the path levels off as it enters a truly magnificent subalpine meadow replete with beaver ponds and lush grasses and shadowed by Thunderbolt Peak

(11,938 feet) to the north and Mount Achonee (12,649 feet) to the south. As the trail ascends from this little hanging valley, the predominant lodgepole pine stand is gradually replaced by Englemann spruce and subalpine fir. At one point, the trail traverses a steep, sunny slope strewn with boulders. After the three log bridges across Pawnee Creek, hikers will find themselves at the Crater Lake Turnoff (6.7 miles).

The left fork at the trail juncture, which is the Cascade Creek Trail, crosses Pawnee Creek and twists up on numerous switchbacks through thick aspen groves and boulder fields. Several rocky outcrops provide good views of Lone Eagle Peak (11,920 feet), Fair Glacier (12,160 feet), and Peck Glacier (11,520 feet) to the south. One sidestream is crossed as the trail climbs through the subalpine forest toward Pawnee Pass. Approximately eight miles up the trail and less than .5 mile from the stream, a side trail leads to the right toward Pawnee Lake (10,840 feet), which is a classic glacial cirque lake surrounded by the jagged slopes of the upper valley and the Continental Divide.

The remaining 2.5 miles to the pass are extremely difficult. Almost thirty switchbacks are encountered in the ascent. The climb is hard, but the view on top is spectacular—one of the best in the entire Indian Peaks. The Great Plains and all of the St. Vrain drainage are visible to the east, including the backside of the Flatirons above Boulder. To the west is an unsurpassed view back down the valley toward Middle Park.

6. CRATER LAKE TRAIL

Trailhead elevation: 10,120 feet
Total vertical ascent: 200 feet
Trail ending: 10,320 feet
Length: 1.1 miles (1.9 kilometers)
Recommended season: July 1 to September 15
Use: Heavy
Difficulty: Difficult
USGS maps: Monarch Lake
Trail profile:

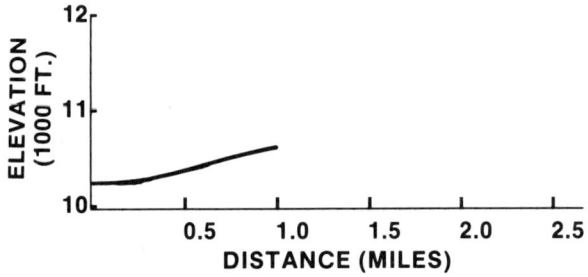

Access:

Follow the Cascade Creek Trail east from Monarch Lake into the wilderness for 6.7 miles. A sign indicates the proper turnoff to the right immediately after the first crossing of Pawnee Creek.

Because of the spectacular setting of Crater Lake—at the foot of Lone Eagle Peak (11,920 feet), a rugged spire rising from the lake's eastern shore—this area is extremely popular, and much environmental damage has occurred

Lone Eagle Peak (11,900 feet) towers above the Douglas fir of the subalpine forest below Crater Lake (10,320 feet). Courtesy U.S. Forest Service.

around the lake. Rangers strictly enforce the regulation prohibiting camping and fires within 100 feet of the lake. A few camping sites can be found lower around Mirror Lake (11,020 feet) or along the trail. Fishing can be good at times both on the stream and in the lakes, but usually not until later in the season. Hikers can also travel cross-country into the upper drainage to visit Triangle Lake (11,120 feet) and even the backside of Lone Eagle Peak. Several people have been killed climbing Lone Eagle Peak in the past few years. It is estimated that 5,000 people visit this backcountry site each year, some just to marvel at Lone Eagle Peak, which ascends some 1,580 feet directly up from the shores of the lake.

The Crater Lake Trail branches off the Cascade Creek Trail rather abruptly and travels up a moderate grade through a classic subalpine forest. There are many

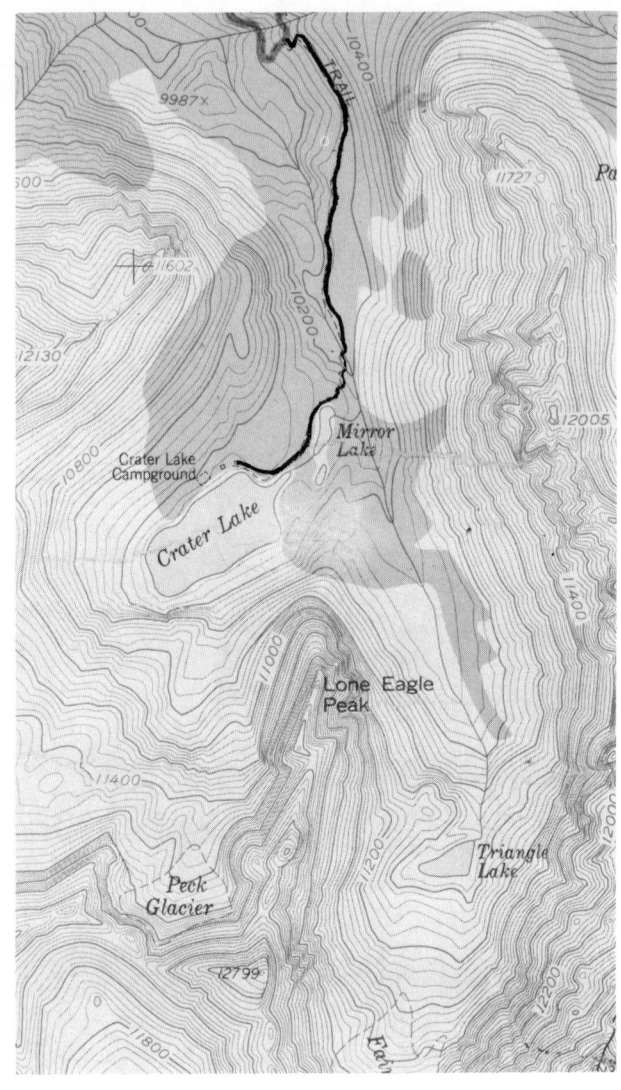

extremely large boulders and slabs of rock, most of which afford a good view of Lone Eagle Peak, Fair Glacier, and Peck Glacier. Shortly after, the trail approaches the creek and follows it for a distance as the clear water drifts through deep, grassy banks and pools surrounding the large boulders.

On hot summer days, in the more private stretches of this stream, both the male and female rosy-bottomed skinny dipper can be observed frolicking in the shallows. They are best left undisturbed, as they are shy and easily startled.

After .6 mile, the trail crosses the stream over a log footbridge and continues on up through the woods. Following a series of switchbacks, the trail levels out at Mirror Lake, which affords a good shot (particularly with a wide-angle lens) of probably the most dramatic scene in the Indian Peaks. It is a good place to take a memorable photograph of a favored companion, with the towering Lone Eagle Peak reflected in the waters of Mirror Lake and the dark forest all around, crowding a rugged shoreline strewn with boulders.

Crater Lake is reached shortly thereafter. On the western shore are the remains of an old log cabin of unknown ancestry. Much of the native wildlife in this remote place is quite tame as a result of the many visitors. Birds, squirrels, and chipmunks will surely visit your campsite begging for small crumbs. Bats are commonly seen over the lake at night, darting about erratically as they feed on the mosquitoes and small hatches rising from the surface. Pikas and marmots can also be seen in the rockslides, scurrying and foraging from hole to hole with their little mouths stuffed full of grass, busily preparing for the long winter ahead.

7. HELL CANYON TRAIL

Trailhead elevation: 8,640 feet
Total vertical ascent: 1,320 feet
Trail ending: 9,960 feet
Length: 1.9 miles (3.1 kilometers)
Recommended season: July 1 to September 15
Use: Light
Difficulty: Difficult
USGS maps: Monarch Lake and Isolation Peak
Trail profile:

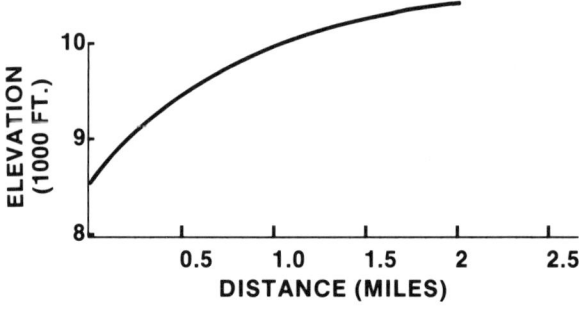

Access:

> There are two ways to reach Hell Canyon. (1) Most easy is to hike up the Cascade Creek Trail for 2.3 miles to the trail junction designated on the left by the Hell Canyon Trail sign. (2) More adventurous is to follow the Roaring Fork Trail to Stone Lake and then hike southwest down Hell Canyon to Long Lake, where the maintained trail can be found on the right-hand or western shoreline.

Hell Canyon is appropriately named, and it is a good trail for the experienced backcountry traveler who desires a truly pristine wilderness experience. Because of its rugged

Many cascades and waterfalls are found in the first mile of the Hell Canyon Trail. Courtesy Charles W. Murray, Jr.

and remote character, it is one of the least visited drainages in the Indian Peaks, offering good camping and fishing, quiet forests, numerous waterfalls and cascades, serene lakes, and scenic mountains. Winter lingers long in the drainage because of the close canyon walls and high altitude, and it is prudent to wait until the Fourth of July or later before venturing up the trail.

The hike itself is only for the extremely fit. A kind of primitive darwinism operates on the trail, with the weak turning back for more gentle terrain and the tough continuing on into the canyon. The trail is poorly defined and is often lost in the forest, adding to the challenge. Beginning with a steep incline, the trail continues to be difficult all the way up the canyon to Long Lake. Approximately one mile from the trailhead, the path enters a steep boulder field which reminds me of the grueling hill

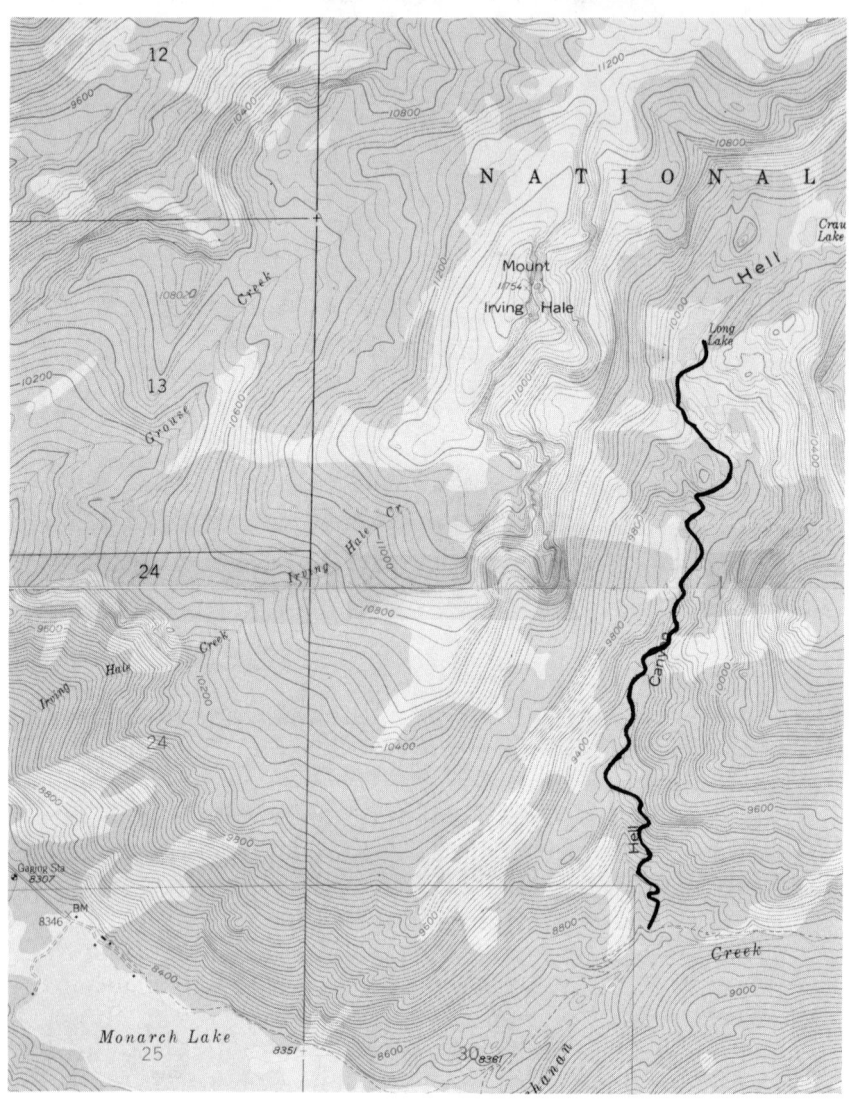

trail through which all Marine officer candidates must pass at Quantico—each one worse than the last. Rock cairns help to identify the trail through this stretch, and at one point the trail squeezes between a narrow, cave-like passageway between the boulders. At mile 1.9, the trail suddenly comes upon Long Lake, which is only five acres in size and very shallow. The best camping is on the eastern shoreline, where both flat terrain and protective forest are found. On the western shores is a large boulder field at the base of Mount Irving Hale (11,754 feet).

Following a faint trail that begins at the far end of Long Lake, you can then hike more or less cross-country further up into the drainage toward Crawford and Stone Lake. Beyond Stone Lake, and 1.7 miles above Long Lake, is Upper Lake. All of these lakes are pretty, set as they are in tundra and deep grass meadows, with the grass often waist high. Stone Lake is particularly striking, set as it is between Hiamovi Mountain (12,041 feet). Wild flowers abound in the subalpine and alpine meadows of this area, include snowlillies, globeflowers, marshmarigolds, elephantella, lupine, and purple fringe. It goes without saying that deer and elk are abundant in Upper Hell Canyon and that trout are also plentiful.

The U.S. Forest Service deleted the Hell Canyon Trail from the system in 1986. This means that the trail still exists, but that it is not being actively maintained. The result will be that Hell Canyon will gradually be returned to a primordial condition, offering wilderness travelers a greater challenge. Hikers should check with the office in Granby, or with the Forest Service volunteer at Monarch Lake, before setting off into this remote and wild canyon.

8. BUCHANAN PASS TRAIL

Trailhead elevation: 8,820 feet
Total vertical ascent: 3,017 feet
Trail ending: 11,837 feet
Length: 5.9 miles (9.5 kilometers)
Recommended season: July 1 to September 15
Use: Heavy
Difficulty: Moderate
USGS maps: Monarch Lake and Isolation Peak
Trail profile:

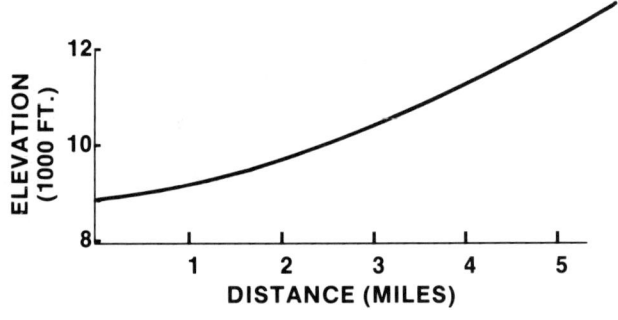

Access:

The Buchanan Trail is easily found 3.3 miles up the Cascade Creek Trail, a short distance beyond Shelter Rock. Take the left fork. The right fork continues up the Cascade Creek drainage.

Like the Cascade Creek Trail, which terminates on Pawnee Pass, the Buchanan Pass Trail offers the backcountry traveler the unique opportunity to cross over the Continental Divide from west to east or east to west, and

Fox Park, seen here in the early summer, is found on Upper Buchanan Creek. Courtesy U.S. Forest Service.

thus to observe the Indian Peaks in all of their splendor and variety. The Buchanan Pass Trail provides not only the usual spectacular scenery of the upper glacial valleys, but abundant wildlife in the form of deer and elk, and generally excellent fishing in its waters. The actual pass, like Pawnee, Arapaho, Devil's Thumb, and Rollins passes, is usually snowcovered until at least the Fourth of July and some years for a week or two beyond that date.

The Buchanan Pass Trail begins in a lodgepole pine forest where the blueberry patches are thick above loudly rushing Buchanan Creek. After .75 mile, the trail comes level with the creek as the water swirls in a maelstrom

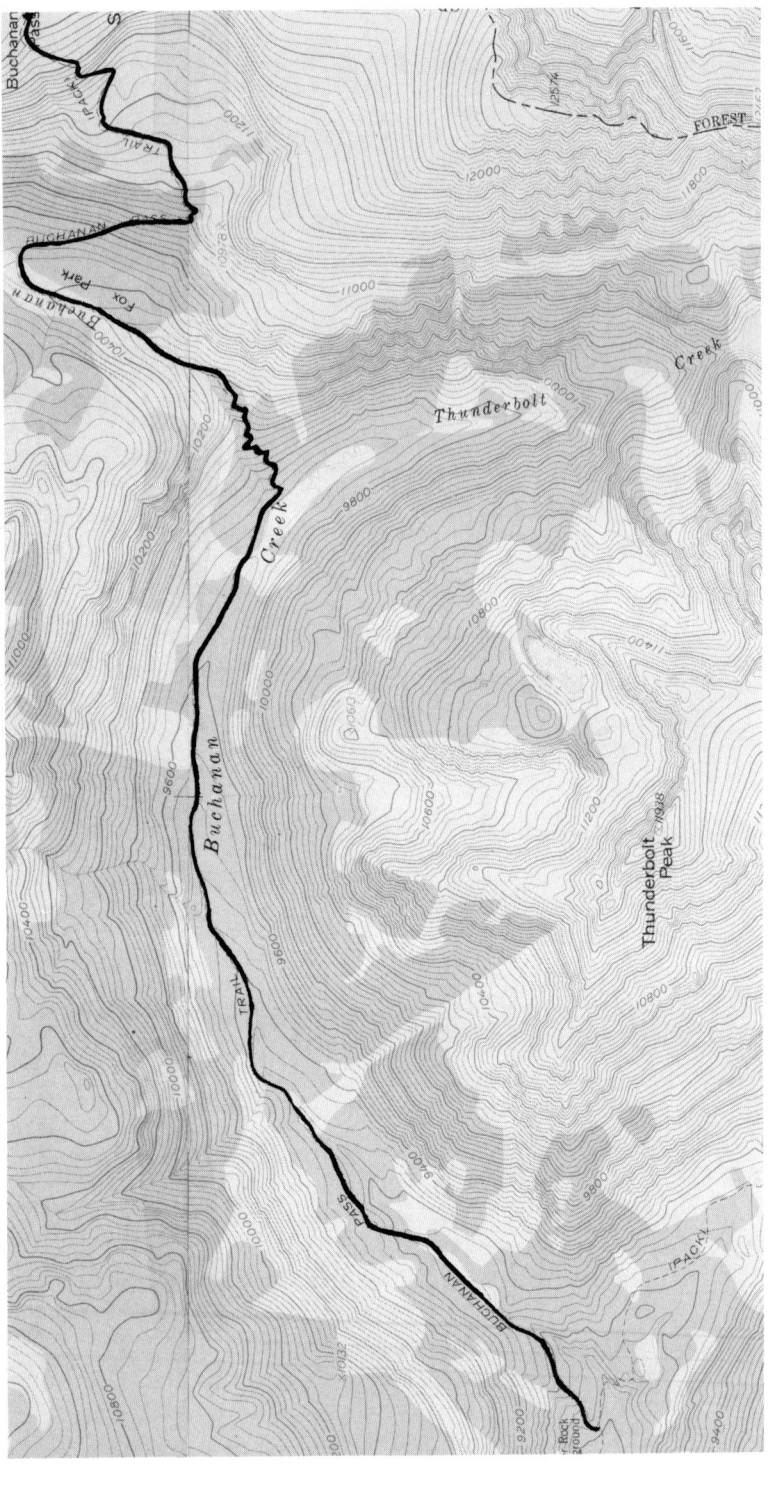

around large boulders and log jams. Shortly thereafter, the water becomes more subdued in an open area of small meadows and ponds created by beavers, the civil engineers of the wilderness. For the next mile to the Gourd Lake turnoff, the trail gradually climbs parallel to the creek. Thunderbolt Peak looms off to the right. The trail crosses a small stream that originates at Gourd Lake just past the turnoff.

Beyond the Gourd Lake turnoff, the trail is relatively level until it crosses Buchanan Creek on the log bridge at Thunderbolt Valley. The switchbacks above this point become quite steep and rugged. Once across the next bridge (3.6 miles from the trailhead), the trail wanders through several groves of subalpine fir and meadows of alpine willow. Soon the wild flowers begin to dominate the ground underfoot, and the firs recede to the far edges of what is now Fox Park. In summer, Fox Park lends itself to photography with its numerous wildflowers such as snowlilly, larkspur, lupine, monkshood, Indian paintbrush, and American bistort in the foreground providing a sharp contrast to the surrounding terrain of the divide.

Some 1,400 feet above Fox Park is Buchanan Pass, reached after climbing the remaining two miles of trail through subalpine forest that at last gives way to krummholz and alpine tundra. Several switchbacks lead up the last rocky slope of the pass, providing a fine view of Sawtooth Mountain (12,304 feet) and the Middle St. Vrain Valley to the east, and, on a clear day, of the Great Plains beyond. To the west is the dramatic lower Buchanan and Cascade valleys. As is the case in all of the more remote upper drainages, deer and elk are often seen around dawn and dusk. If you see a furry little fellow peering over a spruce deadfall at your camp some night, it is probably the omnipresent pine marten, who calls this part of the mountains home. Very curious but shy, he will be gone before you can reach for your camera.

9. GOURD LAKE TRAIL

Trailhead elevation: 9,250 feet
Total vertical ascent: 1,550 feet
Trail ending: 10,800 feet
Length: 2.7 miles (4.3 kilometers)
Recommended season: July 1 to September 15
Use: Medium
Difficulty: Difficult
USGS maps: Monarch Lake and Isolation Peak
Trail profile:

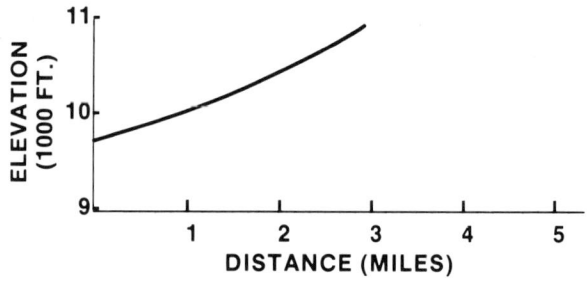

Access:

Follow the Cascade Creek Trail to a signed trail junction just past Shelter Rock. Take the Buchanan Pass Trail for 2.25 miles to where a sign on the left marks the trailhead.

The Gourd Lake Trail is very steep with countless switchbacks. The climb can be very tiring, even to those in shape, when carrying a heavy backpack. Few good camping sites are available at Gourd Lake. The best are found on the

A quiet inlet of Gourd Lake, (10,800 feet), with Thunderbolt Peak (11,938 feet) in the far background. Courtesy U.S. Forest Service.

south, east, and north shores, as well as around the pond below. The lake can remain frozen until well after July 1, but when it does open, the fishing is excellent. Cross-country hikes can be made above Gourd Lake to Island Lake or Fox Park. There are no established trails in the upper drainage, however.

The trail begins on the Buchanan Pass trail and almost immediately you encounter the long switchbacks that make this hike rather strenuous. Most switchbacks are in sight of one another, but short-cuts should be avoided. Most of the ascent is through a lodgepole pine forest. Both sides of the trail are thick with blueberries—a favored late summer and fall food for black bears (be on the lookout for them). Several rocky openings along the way provide an awesome view of Thunderbolt Peak (11,938 feet), across

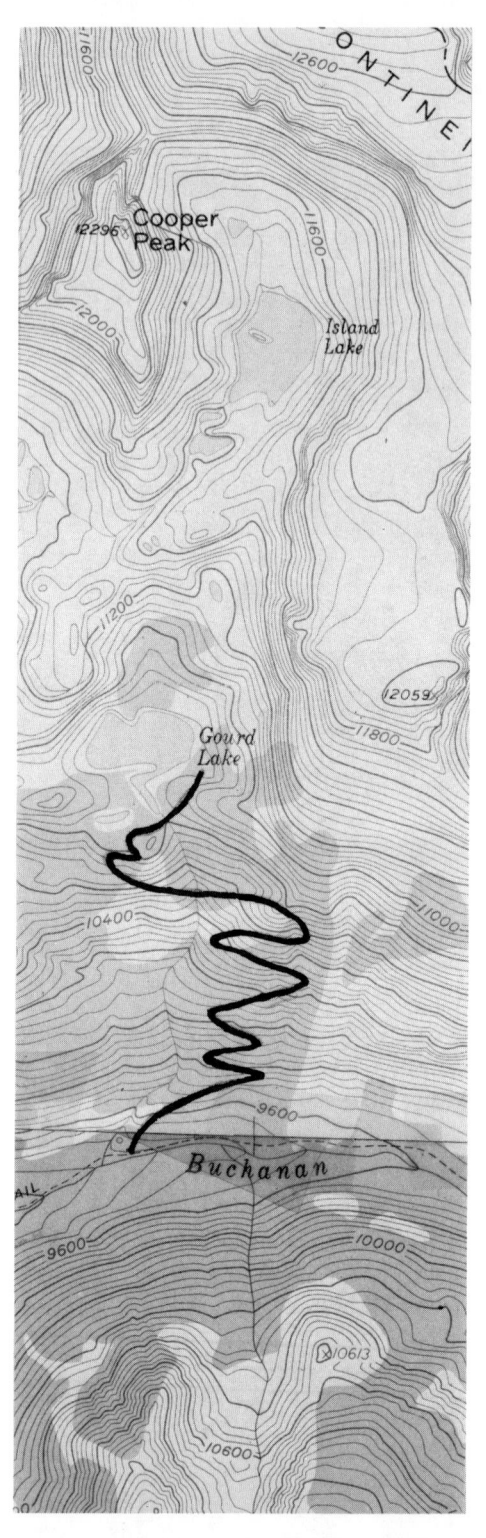

the Buchanan Creek Valley. Upvalley and to the east are Paiute Peak (13,088 feet) and double-capped Mount Toll (12,979 feet). At one juncture in the trail, the lush green meadow and meandering stream of Thunderbolt Meadow are visible at the base of Paiute Peak.

The first series of switchbacks ends mercifully at the first stream crossing. Four more rather diminutive streams are crossed as the lodgepole begin to give way to subalpine forest. A second set of switchbacks leads up to a picturesque pond directly below Gourd Lake, which is a good place to camp if the lakeshores above are too crowded or noisy. The trail then crosses the small stream flowing from the pond and follows the left shoreline to Gourd Lake.

Gourd Lake is nestled between Marten Peak (12,041 feet) to the northwest, Cooper Peak (12,296 feet) to the north, and the Continental Divide to the northeast. The southeastern shores are more or less well fronted with trees and coves, whereas the northwestern shoreline consists of steep rock faces and talus slides. A good view of the surrounding Indian Peaks can be had from the cliffs on the north shore. At this spot you can sometimes see, on a clear day, the snowcapped mountains of the Gore Range far to the south. Deer and elk are found in abundance in the upper drainage, and fish are plentiful.

10. ROARING FORK TRAIL

Trailhead elevation: 8,300 feet
Total vertical ascent: 2,343 feet
Trail ending: 10,643 feet
Length: 6 miles (9.7 kilometers)
Recommended season: July 1 to September 15
Use: Moderate
Difficulty: Difficult
USGS maps: Isolation Peak and Shadow Mountain
Trail profile:

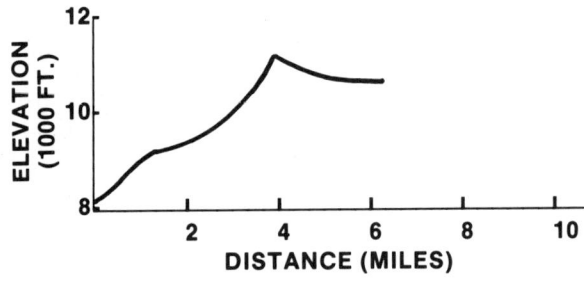

Access:

Take Highway 34 to county road 6 and turn right or east. Follow this unpaved road 9.4 miles along Granby Reservoir to Monarch Lake. Take the Roaring Fork Loop to the Arapaho Bay Ranger Station. The trailhead is located behind the Arapaho Bay forest service residence.

The Roaring Fork Trail is not one of the more popular trails in the wilderness and is a good way to reach Watanga Lake and the Upper Hell Canyon region, including popular

A spectacular view looking east from the saddle just north of Mount Irving Hale (11,754 feet). Courtesy U.S. Forest Service.

fishing areas like Stone, Crawford, and Long lakes. Excellent backcountry camping sites can be found in several locations, and there is an abundance of elk and deer along the entirety of the trail. Fine views are offered both beneath Mount Irving Hale (11,754 feet) and in the vicinity of Stone Lake, which can be put to good use by the poet, artist, or photographer.

The most difficult section of the Roaring Fork Trail is the very first mile, so don't be discouraged. It does get better. From the trailhead in the creek bottom, the path steeply ascends several switchbacks through a thick forest of spruce and lodgepole pine. Not far away, and off to the left, the Roaring Fork Creek can be heard as it loudly cascades

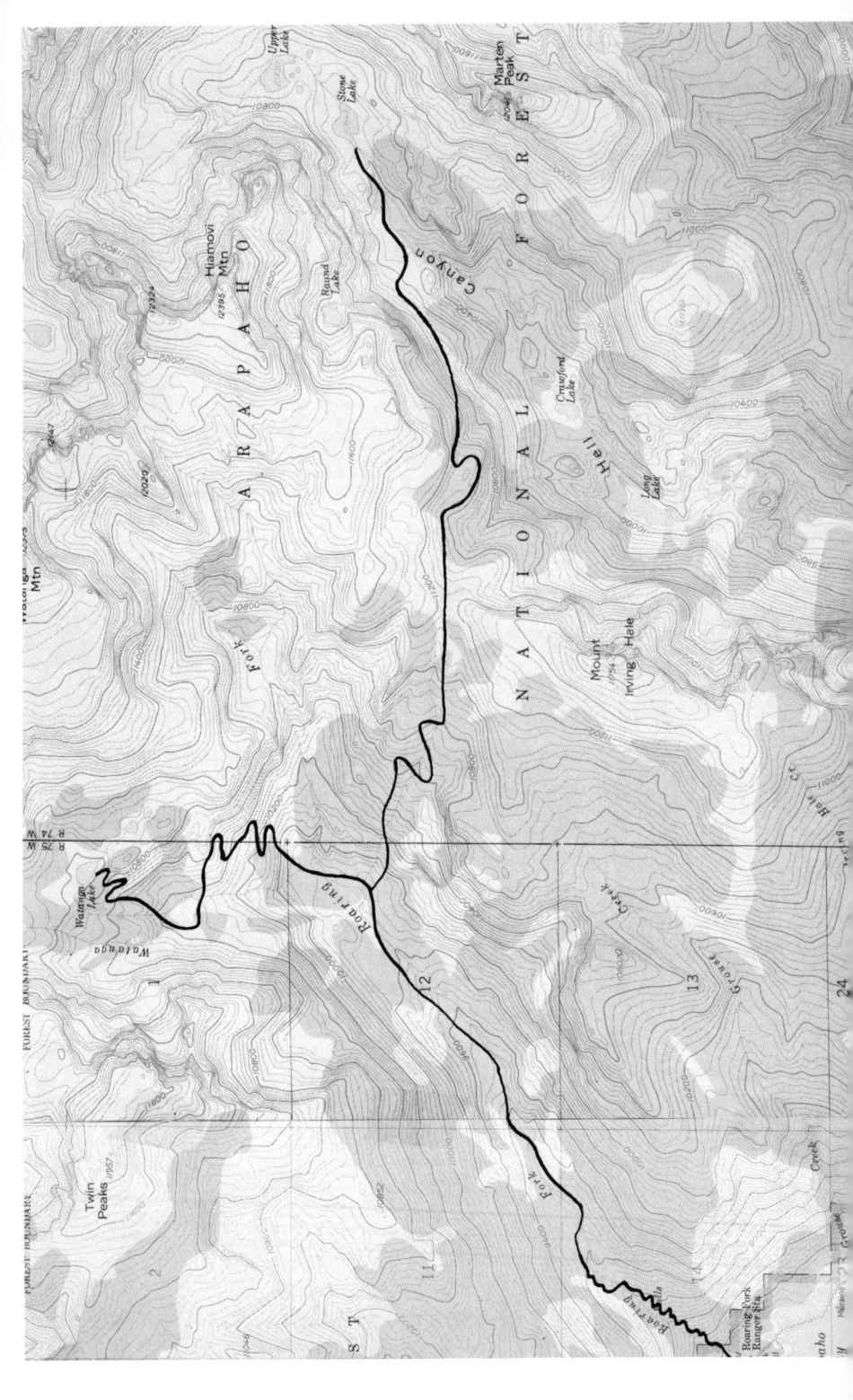

over a series of small waterfalls, large boulders, and log jams down toward Granby Reservoir. The trail follows the creek, now on the west side, for 1.5 miles until the second log footbridge is crossed.

Following this crossing, the trail divides, the left fork leading to Watanga Lake (10,790 feet) and the right continuing on to Stone Lake (10,643 feet). Soon the right fork enters a thick subalpine forest as it climbs steeply in a southeasterly direction. After crossing several small meadows, the trail leads to the top of a saddle at the base of Mount Irving Hale (11,754 feet). This is the highest point reached on the trail (11,200 feet), and the view of the Indian Peaks, the distant Gore Range, and the Vasquez Range is striking. About .75 mile below the saddle, the trail passes an old sheepherder's cabin, now in a state of decay and a favorite haunt of porcupines, and then steeply descends the long rocky ridge leading toward Stone Lake. As the trail makes its final approach to Stone Lake, it begins to fade, but several rock cairns help the traveler keep his or her bearings.

The U.S. Forest Service deleted the Watanga Lake Trail from the system in 1986. This means that the trail still exists, but that it is not being actively maintained. This region will slowly be returned to more primitive conditions, thus providing wilderness hikers with a greater challenge. Hikers should check with the office in Granby, or with the Forest Service volunteer at Monarch Lake, before setting off on the Watanga Lake Trail.

11. KNIGHT RIDGE TRAIL

Trailhead elevation: 8,300 feet
Total vertical ascent: 580 feet (over Twin Pines Point)
Trail ending: 8,300 feet (Twin Creek patrol cabin in national park)
Length: 4.3 miles (6.9 kilometers)
Recommended season: June 10 to September 30
Use: Light
Difficulty: Easy
USGS maps: Isolation Peak and Shadow Mountain
Trail profile:

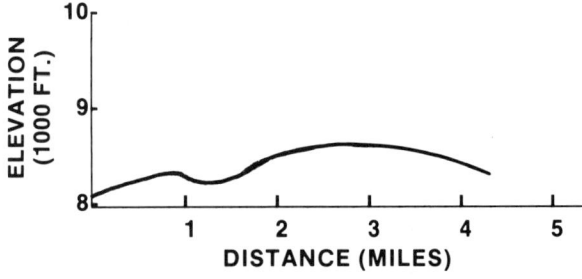

Access:

>Same road access as trail number 10 (Roaring Fork Trail). West from Roaring Fork Campground over Roaring Fork Creek.

Probably the least major of any trail that claims to be part of the Indian Peaks Wilderness, this trail simply connects the Twin Creek patrol cabin in Rocky Mountain National Park along Grand Bay, an inlet of Lake Grandby, with the Roaring Fork Campground. It is frequently used by

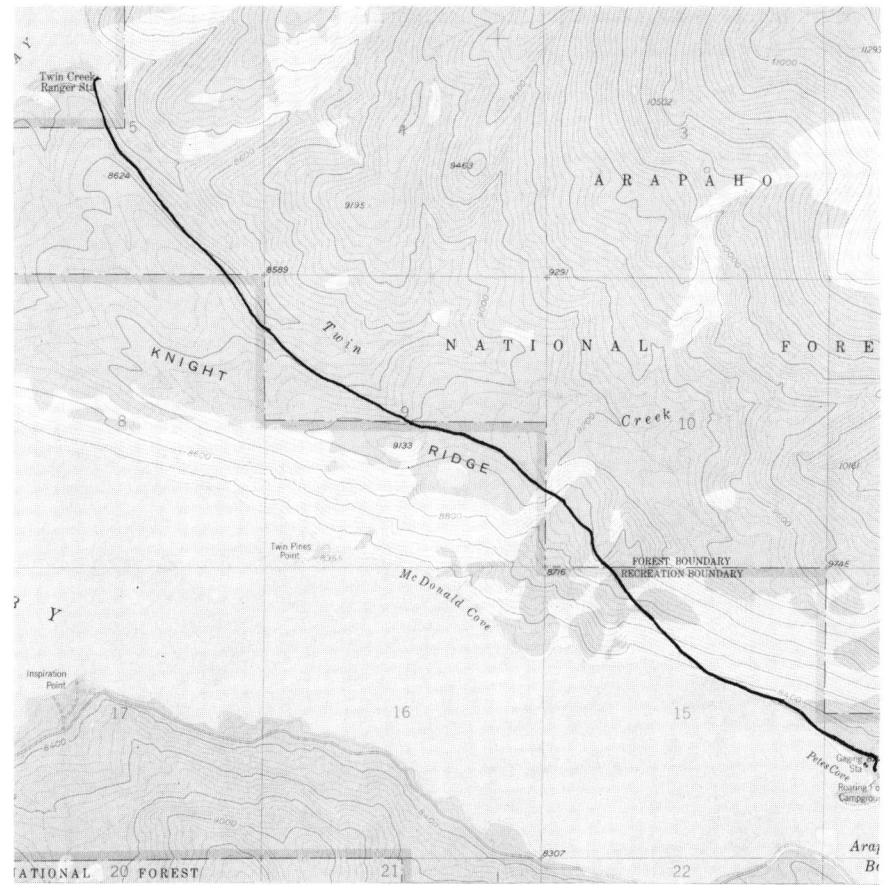

fishermen to reach Pete's Cove and McDonald Cove, along the north shore of the lake beneath Knight Ridge. Approximately 1.3 miles west of the Roaring Fork Campground, the trail begins to ascend Twin Pines Point, climbing 580 feet through sagebrush meadows, steep rockslides, and aspen groves. It crosses Twin Pines Point beside a small pond and then descends along the northwest drainage of Twin Creek through a forest of lodgepole pine to the patrol cabin.

TRAILS EAST OF THE DIVIDE

Some of the finest glacial scenery in the Front Range is found on the east slope of the Indian Peaks. Pictured here is the Continental Divide as seen from Red Rock Lake, on the road to the Long Lake Trailhead. Courtesy Charles W. Murray, Jr.

Trails on the Eastern Slope of the Indian Peaks Wilderness are less centrally located and easily reached than those on the Western Slope and are for the most part far more crowded. In many areas, such as Rainbow Lakes, Brainard Lake, and Buckingham Campground, it is difficult to find parking on weekends and holidays after 10 a.m. in the months of July and August. Several miles back, crowds of people still scurry up and down the trails in a scene reminiscent of the trails in Yosemite Valley, or around Old Faithful in Yellowstone, or on the North Rim of the Grand Canyon. Even the more familiar Maroon Bells of Aspen, a favorite of calendar photographers across the world, have less visitors than some of these drainages. Consequently, the only way to still enjoy a solitary hike is to leave the trailhead just at sunrise. Maintaining a vigorous pace, it is possible to complete most of the circuits up to the divide and back by late in the morning, when the hoards of day hikers from Boulder and Denver are just arriving. On the bright side, the glacial scenery is literally unsurpassed in the Front Range of Colorado, and there are many opportunities, particularly in the morning when the sun is on the back range, to take fine mountain photographs.

Wildlife is very scarce in this region, and some areas, such as the South St. Vrain drainage, are, for all intents and purposes, sterilized in terms of deer and elk. Access is from Colorado 72, which runs north-south parallel to the Continental Divide. All trailheads are reached by taking one of four county roads (116, 102, 130, and 114) off to the west from the main highway.

1. PAWNEE PASS TRAIL

Trailhead elevation: 10,400 feet
Total vertical ascent: 2,141 feet
Trail ending: 12,541 feet
Length: 4.5 miles (7.2 kilometers)
Recommended season: July 1 to September 15
Use: Extremely heavy
Difficulty: Moderate to difficult
USGS maps: Ward and Monarch Lake
Trail profile:

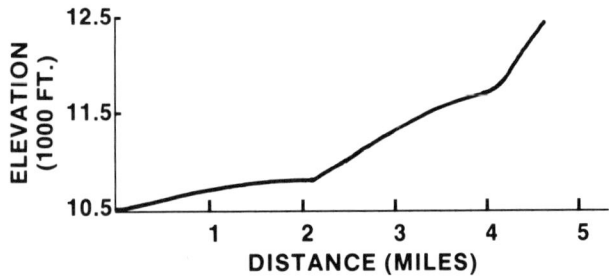

Access:

Take Colorado 72 north of Nederland approximately 13 miles to the town of Ward. Turn left on county road 102 and follow for five miles. The road is closed at the cattleguard three miles west during the winter months because of heavy drifting (fifteen to twenty feet) on the hill just beyond.

If you are looking for solitude and tranquility, this is decidedly not the place to go. The Pawnee Pass Trail is the single most heavily used trail in the Indian Peaks. As a

The trees begin to thin out just at timberline on the Pawnee Pass Trail, above Lake Isabelle. Courtesy Linda Elinoff.

result, much damage has resulted in the fragile subalpine forests and on the tundra. Visitors should be particularly careful as they hike in this region, avoiding shortcuts between switchbacks and observing tightly enforced regulations prohibiting campfires, livestock, and camping.

Parking is always a problem. The parking area at Long Lake, where the trail begins, is reserved exclusively for day hikers. Backpackers should drop their gear at the trailhead and then park back down the road in designated areas, which are usually crowded by midmorning on weekends and holidays in the summer.

The Long Lake to Monarch Lake circuit via Pawnee Pass is one of the best trails to take in the Indian Peaks in terms of scenery. Allow two full days for the fourteen-mile trip, and take at least two rolls of film. The climb to the top of the pass, one of the highest along the entire Continental Divide, is extremely difficult. Hikers from lower elevations commonly develop nosebleeds and headaches and suffer from shortness of breath over the last mile of the ascent.

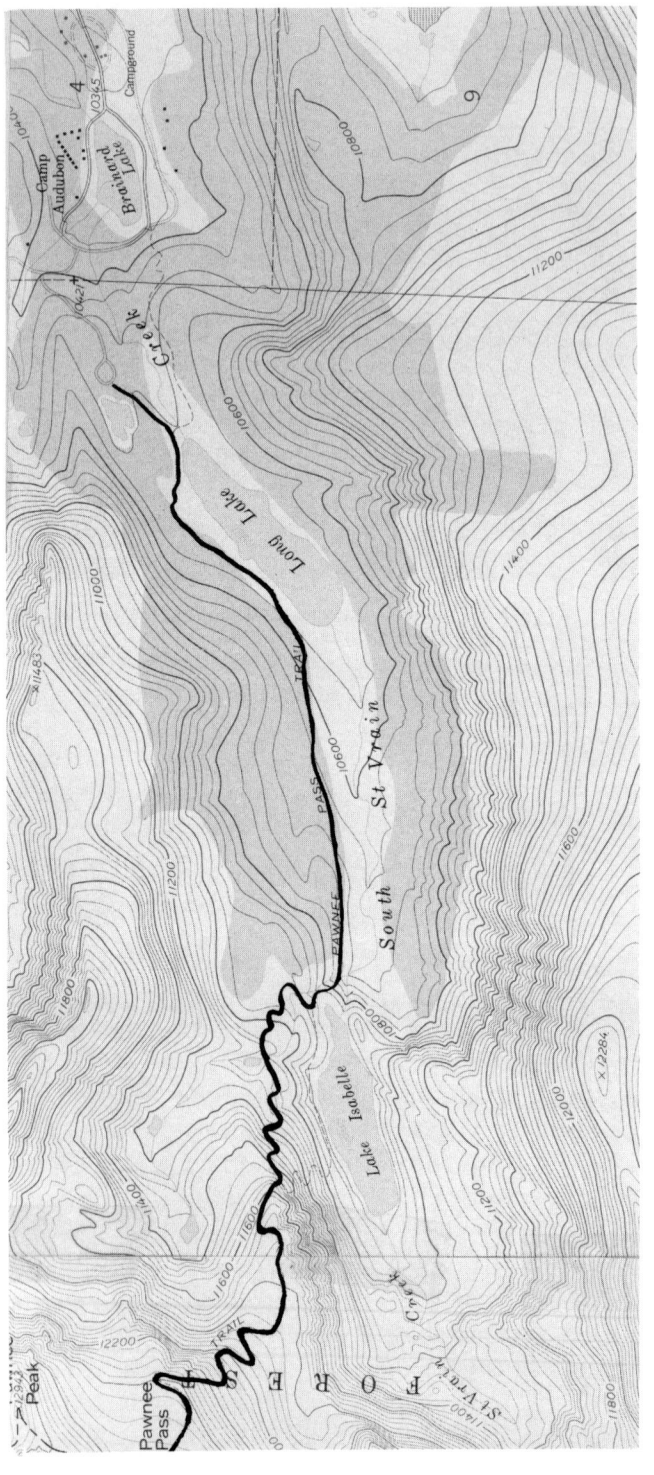

The view looking east from the final approach to Pawnee Pass includes Long Lake and Lefthand Reservoir below Niwot Ridge in the foreground, and the Great Plains in the far background. Courtesy Linda Elinoff.

The trail begins just beyond the outhouses at the southwestern corner of the parking lot and closely parallels South St. Vrain Creek through the very fine forest of subalpine fir and Englemann spruce. Snow sometimes lingers in this dense forest through this dense forest through the middle of July, and some years the pass can not be attempted until that time. Fishing is often good in the creek. Fair-sized brook trout can be found in the quiet pools and are particularly fond of mosquito imitations. Good sports quickly return these wild trout to the waters for others to enjoy.

A dam crosses the creek .25 mile from the trailhead. The path across the dam leads to the Jean Luning Trail, named for a legislative aide to then Representative Tim Wirth who was instrumental in gaining wilderness designation for the Indian Peaks. The trail provides an interesting 2.2 mile circuit around Long Lake.

A few hundred yards down the Jean Luning Trail there is

a fork, with the left fork climbing up Niwot Ridge through the dense north slope subalpine forest, and the right fork continuing on around Long Lake. The only deer and elk sign in the area is found on Niwot Ridge, a relatively wild ridge which has been designated part of the international biosphere by the United Nations for arctic and alpine research. A small research cabin maintained by the University of Colorado can be found further up the ridge, and an extremely obese marmot lives nearby. The cabin and its contents, mostly scientific instruments, should not be disturbed. It is forbidden to cross further south over the ridge into the next watershed, which is part of the water supply for Boulder.

The Pawnee Pass Trail parallels the north shore of Long Lake, passing through bogs, meadows, and subalpine forest for another 1.5 miles. Many beautiful wild flowers are found here, including globeflower and marshmarigold early in the season and shooting star, butter and eggs, paintbrush, larkspur, and columbine later in the summer. Much of this region is successional in nature—the lower forms of vegetation such as moss and liverwort reclaiming what was recently pond and bog. Needless to say, this process takes thousands of years.

Just beyond the western end of Long Lake (where fishing is usually good at the inlet), the trail divides, with the left-hand fork becoming the far end of the Jean Luning Trail, and the right-hand fork ascending toward Lake Isabelle and Pawnee Pass. It is worthwhile to hike down into the meadows at this point and take a few photographs looking upvalley toward the impressive array of peaks, which are, from right to left Pawnee Peak (12,943 feet), Shoshone Peak (12,967 feet), Apache Peak (13,441 feet), Navajo Peak (13,409 feet), and Arikaree Peak (13,156 feet). Even those who have traveled to furthest Nepal claim that this view of the Indian Peaks is one of the loveliest mountain scenes in all the world, with the deeply flowered meadows around the lazy stream in the foreground, the waterfall from Lake Isabelle at mid-distance, and the great jagged peaks in the background.

Looking West from Pawnee Pass (12,550 feet), Lake Granby can be seen at mid-range and the drainage of the Colorado River at extreme distance. Courtesy Linda Elinoff.

The right-hand fork of the trail begins to steeply ascend the subalpine forest at this point. As you near Lake Isabelle, do not cross the creek, but head east (right) into the woods at the trail junction (10,800 feet). The Ward USGS map shows the incorrect configuration here, and at least an hour can be lost wandering around the shores of Lake Isabelle trying to figure out what happened and how to get back on the trail. If you want to see Lake Isabelle, simply take the left-hand fork and you will soon find yourself on the shores of this beautiful (10,868 feet) cirque lake. Fishing can be good here at times. By following the trail around the north shore and into the deep grass meadows surrounding the upper creek, hikers can reach Isabelle Glacier (12,000 feet).

The rest of the Pawnee Pass Trail is pure work, up countless steep switchbacks toward the distant saddle between Pawnee and Shoshone peaks. Shortly after the switchbacks, the trail reaches a bench situated about 1,000 feet above Lake Isabelle, which is set like a jewel in stone in the valley below. The views back downcountry and east over the Great Plains are tremendous. The scenery from the pass itself is even more spectacular, particularly over the extremely rugged country at the headwaters of Pawnee Creek. Most all of the peaks in this region can be climbed, but only Pawnee Peak, which is .5 mile to the north of the pass, is a really safe walk up.

2. MITCHELL LAKE TRAIL

Trailhead elevation: 10,500 feet
Total vertical ascent: 800 feet
Trail ending: 11,300 feet
Length: 2.5 miles (4 kilometers)
Recommended season: July 1 to September 15
Use: Extremely heavy
Difficulty: Moderate
USGS maps: Ward

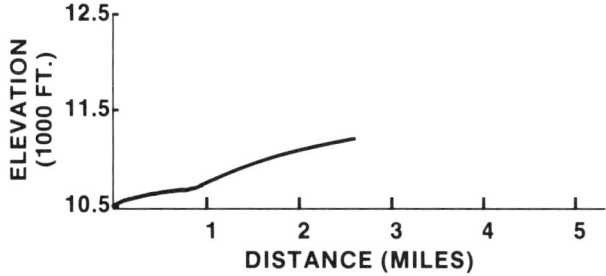

Access:

Turn left (west) on county road 102 (Brainard Lake Road) just north of Ward from Colorado 72. Drive to the Mitchell Lake parking area, which is reserved for day use only, and start out on the trail west of the bulletin board.

The Mitchell Lake Trail, though short, provides an excellent opportunity to those without the time or stamina required by the longer valley trails to experience both the subalpine and the alpine ecosystem in a setting of great natural beauty. It is a favorite of many of the older hikers

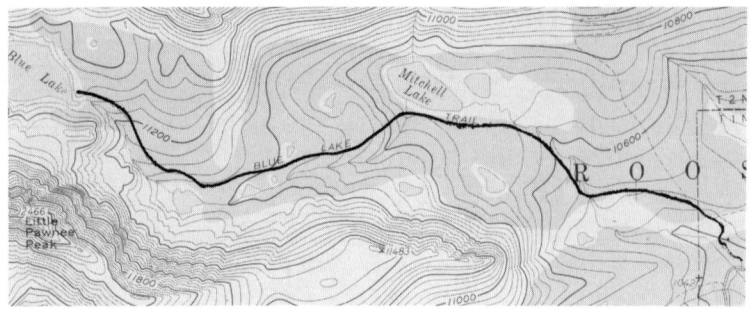

and couples with young children, particularly in the fall, when the tundra begins to change colors and achieve a striking and distinctive quality. Photographers also enjoy this trail for the many fine forest and meadow shots, as well as those which can be taken around the two lakes in the drainage.

The trail begins on the south side of the parking lot. Mitchell Creek, several hundred yards away, can be heard through the forest. The path runs for the most part level through the trees, crosses the creek, then bears to the left and begins to wind uphill to the level of Mitchell Lake (10,720 feet). A good photograph of Mount Audubon (13,223 feet) can be taken in the lower forest, framed between the tall and stately spruce and fir trees, with a companion perhaps in the foreground to emphasize the dramatic size of the country. Mount Toll (12,979 feet) is also visible a half mile to the west of Mount Audubon.

From the lake, the trail ascends parallel to Mitchell Creek toward Blue Lake (11,300 feet), passing through fine forests and meadows as well as several interesting rock outcroppings. Some rock outcroppings in this part of the Rockies are of Precambrian age (roughly one billion years old) and are among the oldest rocks known to man (except those found on the moon). Older rocks have been found, but they are rare, because crustal mineral material is steadily recycled as a result of plate tectonics.

Blue Lake is finally reached at mile 2.5, nestled at the base of several enormous rockslides. The surrounding

Blue Lake (11,300 feet), a short distance above Mitchell Lake (10,400 feet), normally does not open up until after the fourth of July. Courtesy U.S. Forest Service.

peaks, from right to left, are Mount Audubon (13,223 feet), Paiute Peak (13,088 feet), Mount Toll (12,979 feet), Pawnee Peak (12,943 feet), and Little Pawnee Peak (12,466 feet). Mitchell Creek cascades from a shelf 500 feet above Blue Lake, where a third lake or tarn is located called Little Blue Lake (11,833 feet). This lake can be reached by following the faint trail around Blue Lake's northern shore. The trail then climbs to the right of the lovely waterfall. Mount Toll can be ascended by the hardy and careful by climbing through the boulders and rockslides to the southwestern summit. Likewise, an ascent can be made of Paiute Peak. The emphasis in both cases would be on extreme caution, not only with respect to the terrain, but also to the weather, which could trap climbers far above timberline in the midst of an electrical storm.

3. BEAVER CREEK TRAIL

Trailhead elevation: 10,800 feet
Total vertical ascent: 500 feet
Trail ending: 10,400 feet (highest point on trail is 11,300 feet)
Length: 6 miles (9.6 kilometers)
Recommended season: July 1 to September 15
Use: Heavy
Difficulty: Moderate
USGS maps: Ward and Allenspark
Trail profile:

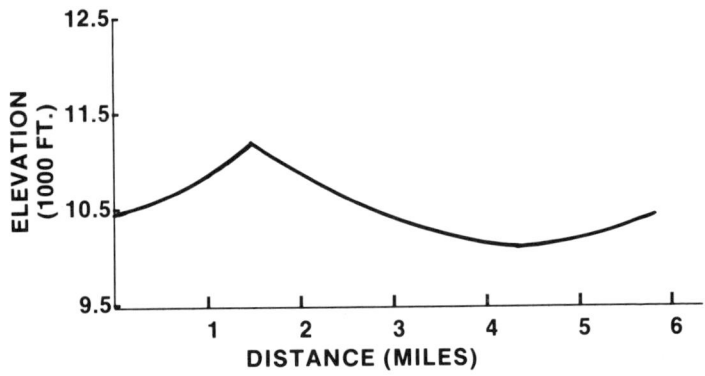

Access:

Same as for Mitchell Lake Trail, except start out north of the Mitchell Lake parking area on the trail marked Mount Audubon/Beaver Creek Trail.

The Beaver Creek Trail is a popular loop trail to travel cross-country from Pawnee Pass and the South St. Vrain drainage to Buchanan Pass and the North St. Vrain drainage. The Ward USGS quadrangle incorrectly identifies the Beaver Creek Trail as the Buchanan Pass Trail.

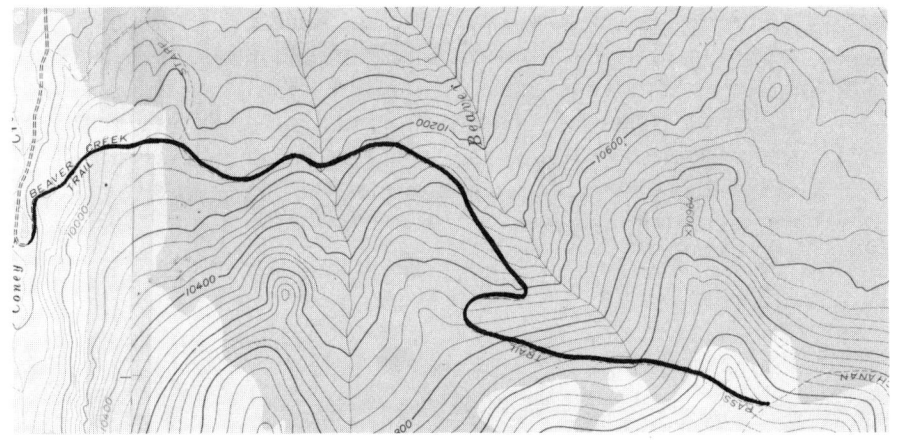

There are many good places to camp once into the North St. Vrain drainage, but campfires are prohibited, so be certain to bring a gas stove.

The trail climbs steadily to the northwest through a dense subalpine forest for .5 mile to a long series of switchbacks. From the western end of the second switchback, there is an excellent view of Mount Toll rising in a brotherly fashion beside and behind the steep upper shoulder of Mount Audubon. The trail switchbacks up the slope through a stand of limber pines, then drops back among the spruce and fir as it nears timberline. The trail separates a short distance above timberline, the right-hand fork being the Beaver Creek Trail and the left-hand fork ascending Mount Audubon.

Soon the Beaver Creek Trail begins its descent from the divide separating the two St. Vrain drainages. There are a few long switchbacks down the gently sloping terrain that is forested with the familiar Englemann spruce, subalpine fir, and occasional limber pine. Campers in these woods will often hear the hooting of the great horned owl in the evening hours, particularly on a night when the moon is close to full phase and the hunting is best. Also, elk can sometimes be heard bugling around timberline in September throughout the Middle St. Vrain drainage.

The trail crosses several branches of Beaver Creek as it continues in a northeasterly direction, finally terminating at Coney Flats, where it is a three-mile hike down the road to Beaver Reservoir. The trail above Beaver Reservoir is not passable to any but four-wheel-drive vehicles. Front-wheel-drive automobiles sometimes can make it, but it is not recommended.

4. MOUNT AUDUBON TRAIL

Trailhead elevation: 11,300 feet (at juncture with Beaver Creek Trail)
Total vertical ascent: 1,933 feet (2,733 feet from Mitchell Lake parking lot)
Trail ending: 13,233 feet
Length: 2 miles (3.2 kilometers)
Recommended season: July 1 to September 15
Use: Extremely heavy
Difficulty: Moderate
USGS maps: Ward
Trail Profile:

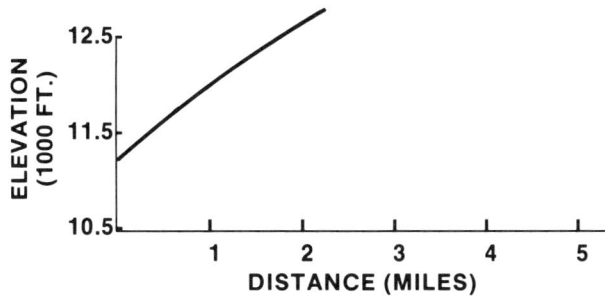

Access:

Same as for Mitchell Lake Trail, except start out north of the Mitchell Lake parking area on the trail marked Mount Audubon/Beaver Creek Trail.

The Mount Audubon Trail is one of the most heavily used trails in the Brainard Lake area and also is one of the most dangerous in terms of exposure to lightning. It is a good rule of thumb to leave the summit no later than noon

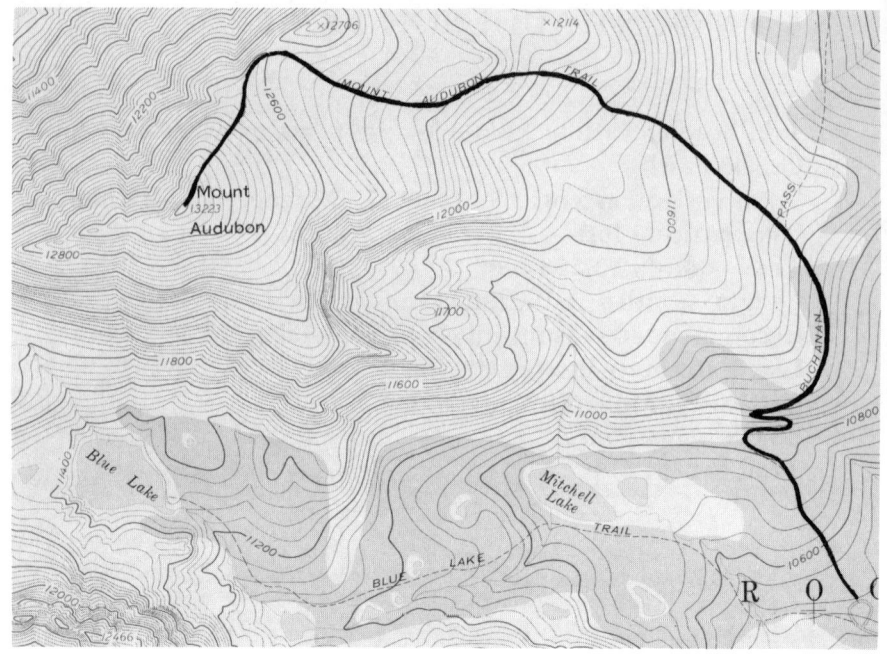

or twelve-thirty in the summer, when convectional storms begin to form around the divide. There is also little water on the trail once above timberline, so carry water and appropriate foul weather gear. If water is drawn from Mitchell Creek before beginning the ascent, it is imperative, as with any water in the Indian Peaks, to use some form of water purification tablets. No water in the wilderness is entirely free anymore of the bacteria and parasites that can cause dysentery.

The trail begins just north of the parking lot. For the first mile hikers take the Beaver Creek Trail, which climbs to 11,300 feet before dropping down into the Middle St. Vrain drainage. A fork in the trail to the northwest leads to the summit of Mount Audubon. Much of the clover on the sides of the trail is not indigenous to the region but apparently was brought here in the droppings of horses before horses were banned from this portion of the wilderness. The clover is flourishing with apparently no ill-effects for the other plants.

The view west from Mount Audubon includes Paiute Peak (13,088 feet) and Upper Coney Lake (10,940 feet). Courtesy U.S. Forest Service.

Following the left fork up toward the summit of Mount Audubon, you will pass through a rich natural garden of tundra wild flowers as you steadily ascend in a northwesterly direction. The terrain is very rocky in places, and many small varieties of cushion plants thrive in the soil around the rocks. At the long saddle to the north of Mount Audubon, the trail turns south and starts up the ridge for the final portion.

In the event of rapidly developing clouds, there are cairns along the way to mark the trail. The terrain to the north and west falls off rather dramatically into the upper Middle St. Vrain drainage and Upper Coney Lake (10,940 feet). The view from the summit of the back range and of the lower country is spectacular.

You have the choice of descending by the same route or ending from Paiute Peak along the obvious routes into the Upper Mitchell Creek drainage. Care should be taken along this descent, as the gullies and couloirs are both rocky and steep. It is an excellent circuit trip and one not often attempted by the average day hiker. It is important to start out early enough to avoid the afternoon thunderstorms.

5. ARAPAHO GLACIER TRAIL
(also known as the Glacier Rim Trail)

Trailhead elevation: 10,000 feet (at Rainbow Lakes Campground)
Total vertical ascent: 12,700 feet
Trail ending: 12,700 feet
Length: 6 miles (11.2 kilometers)
Recommended season: July 1 to September 15
Use: Heavy
Difficulty: Moderate
USGS maps: Nederland and Monarch Lake
Trail profile:

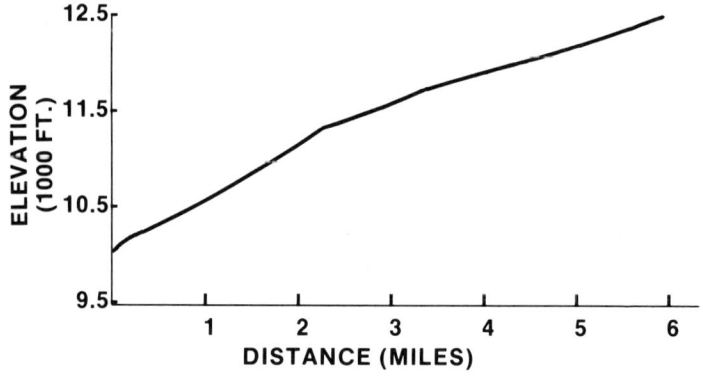

Access:

Rainbow Lakes Campground is reached by driving eight miles north of Nederland and turning left on the road identified as that leading to the University of Colorado Mountain Research Station (County Road 116). After almost a mile, the road forks, with the right fork leading to the University Research Station and the left fork leading to the campground, approximately five miles farther.

As early as the 1920s, people from Boulder and Denver were coming to the lovely Arapaho Glacier to have their photographs taken near the snow in the summertime. The drainage itself is now off-limits to foot travel, as it has been since designated the water source for the City of Boulder. However, hikes can still be made to the magnificent overlook south of the glacier.

The trailhead is located in the vicinity of Rainbow Lakes, which are well stocked and provide fairly good, though for some overly civilized, trout fishing. A vast network of trails connects these lakes, which number almost a dozen.

The Arapaho Glacier Trail begins either from the Fourth of July Mine west of Eldora or, more commonly, from the Rainbow Lakes. The trailhead at Rainbow Lakes begins at the northwestern side of the campground, climbing rather steeply and suddenly through the forest, then leveling out more or less along the fence marking the southern edge of the City of Boulder land. About one mile from the trailhead, the path turns to the left (south) and begins to switchback toward timberline.

As you come out on the tundra, beautiful views are afforded of the South Fork of the North Boulder Creek drainage. Both North Arapaho Peak (13,502 feet) and Arikaree Peaks (13,150 feet) are clearly visible along the divide. During college days at Boulder, we often hiked to this ridge above timberline in mid-August to watch the spectacular meteor shower that occurs every year in the vicinity of the sky known as the Pleiades (a small cluster of stars near Orion). Sometimes we would see as many as thirty of these meteors every minute, streaking across the sky like fireworks. Beyond the lights of the city, they were even more lovely and impressive. Some scientists now believe that some of the important building blocks of life, perhaps even life itself, first came to Earth inside meteorites that crumbled on impact and spread their contents into the primordial seas and terrestrial backwaters about 3 billion years ago. Many complex hydrocarbon molecules have been discovered inside meteorites that geologists have recovered from remote

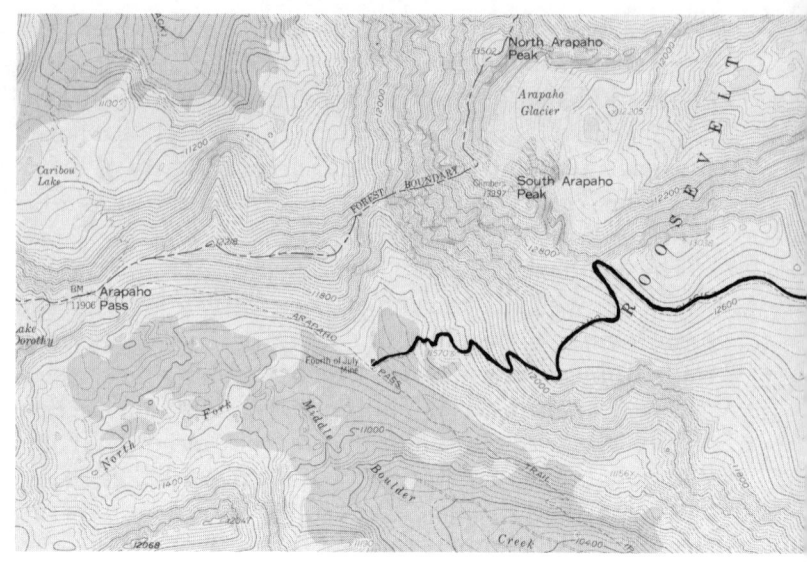

North Arapaho Peak (13,-502 feet), as seen from the Arapaho Glacier Trail. Courtesy U.S. Forest Service.

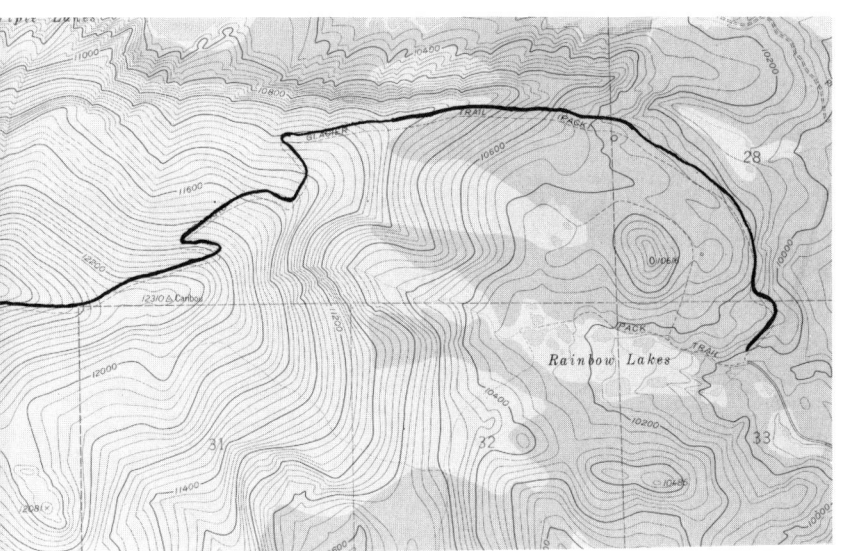

parts of the planet, as well as from the moon.

Through wide switchbacks, the trail winds up the tundra slope north of Caribou, which was at one time an important mining town, but which is now abandoned. An important recording studio has been built on private land in the valley, and many famous rock musicians now record their music in the seclusion and natural beauty of the unique ranch. Caribou Peak (12,310 feet) is a few hundred yards to the south and easily "climbed."

For the next few miles, the path wanders in a westerly direction over the tundra toward the juncture with another trail ascending from the North Fork of Middle Boulder Creek. This juncture affords a good view of Arapaho Glacier, which has the distinction of being the southernmost glacier in North America. Views, especially to the south and west, are simply marvelous on a clear day. Buckingham Campground, down in the drainage of the North Fork of Middle Boulder Creek, is 3.5 miles away, about one-half the distance back to the Rainbow Lakes Campground. Throughout the entire hike, be on the lookout for convectional storms, particularly after noon in the summertime.

6. ARAPAHO PASS TRAIL

Trailhead elevation: 10,121 feet
Total vertical ascent: 1,779 feet
Trail ending: 11,900 feet
Length: 1.5 miles (4.8 kilometers)
Recommended season: July 1 to September 15
Use: Extremely heavy
Difficulty: Moderate
USGS maps: Nederland and Monarch Lake
Trail profile:

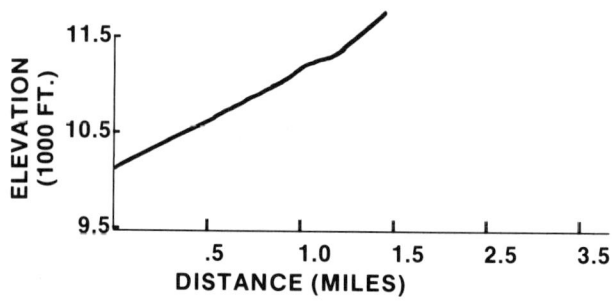

Access:

A few hundred yards south of Nederland on Colorado 72, turn right (west) on the road to the Eldora Ski Area. Drive past the turnoff to the ski area and through Eldora, and past the turnoff to the abandoned 1890s mining camp of Hessie, before coming to the Buckingham/Fourth of July Campground. The total distance is approximately ten miles. The road is rough for the last four miles.

Actually, several minor trails begin at the Buckingham/Fourth of July Campground, only one of

The ascent of Arapaho Pass is usually not feasible until after the Fourth of July. Courtesy U.S. Forest Service.

which is the Arapaho Pass Trail. There is also the Arapaho Glacier Trail on the ridge above and the Diamond Lake Trail, which travels south over the ridge into the South Fork of Middle Boulder Creek and which also connects with the Chittenden Mountain Trail (the Chittenden trail is not signed on the ground at any point and is not recommended for backcountry travel). The area around the campground, including the trails, has been heavily used for many decades, and resource damage has been extreme. It is not an area recommended for those seeking a pristine wilderness experience.

The Arapaho Pass Trail begins at the northwest end of the campground. About two miles up the trail, which parallels the North Fork of Middle Boulder Creek through a subalpine forest and several meadows, the Diamond Lake Trail forks to the left. The entire first 1.2 miles of this trail

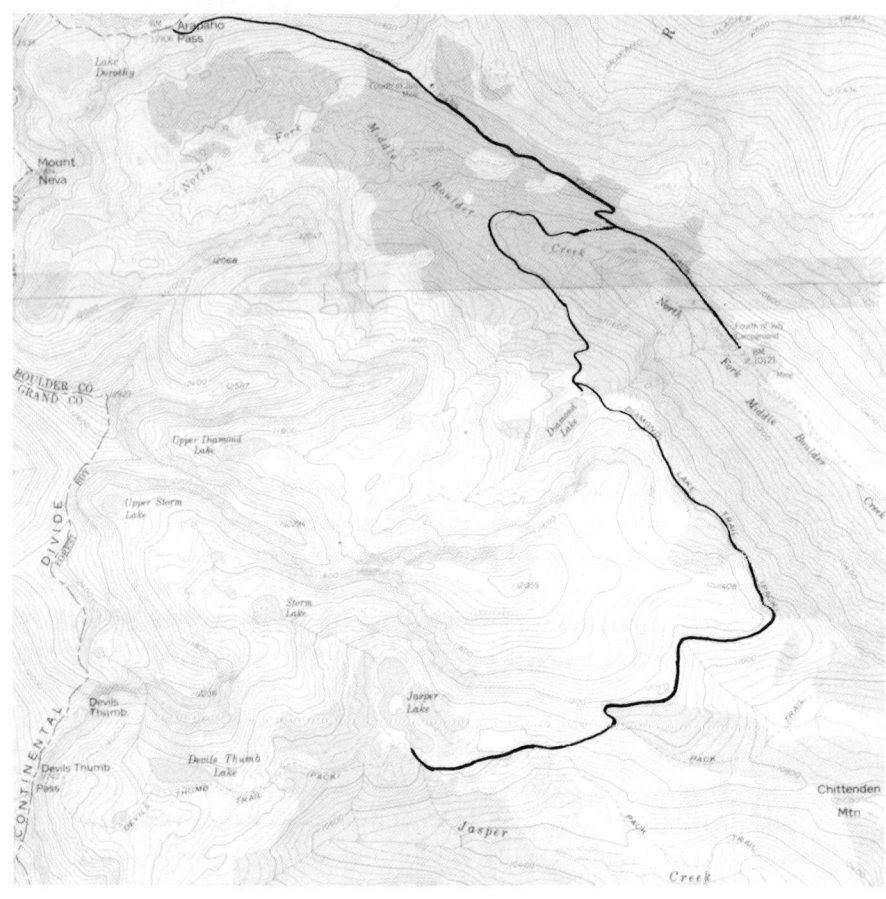

have recently been relocated higher on the slope to bypass private property in the valley bottom. The trail follows an old wagon road for part of its length. At 11,200 feet, the trail visits the famous Fourth of July Mine. From the top of the pass, you can drop into Caribou Lake (11,147 feet) on the other side of the divide. Continuing southwest over Caribou Pass, Columbine Lake (11,040 feet) can be reached. The views from the pass both east and west are excellent.

Arapaho Glacier can be reached either by taking the steep trail up from the Fourth of July Mine or by beginning from the Rainbow Lakes. Either way, the trail is almost

Upper Diamond Lake (11,680 feet) can be reached via the Arapaho Pass trailhead. Courtesy U.S. Forest Service.

entirely above timberline. Be alert for late afternoon storms in the summer. From the glacier overlook, South Arapaho Peak (13,197 feet) can be conquered by those of the boulder-hopping school of mountain climbing.

Back at the juncture with the Diamond Lake Trail, the left fork soon crosses the creek and wanders upward through a dense subalpine forest, skirting several bogs, for another mile before reaching the lake. Considerable destruction has occurred around the lake as a result of overuse. Beyond Diamond Lake, the trail ascends a tundra ridge separating Jasper Creek and the North Fork at 11,400 feet before descending toward its juncture with the Chittenden Mountain Trail and the Devil's Thumb Trail.

The Chittenden Mountain Trail has both its origins and the greater portion of its length outside the wilderness area. It begins north of Hessie, some two miles downcountry through the spruce/fir and lodgepole pine forests, and is used primarily for more direct access to fishing at Jasper Reservoir than can be afforded from the north or south. The juncture with the Devil's Thumb Trail, which leads to Devil's Thumb Pass, occurs about 2.3 miles from Diamond Lake. The ultimate source of the Devil's Thumb Trail is at Hessie.

7. KING LAKE TRAIL

Trailhead elevation: 9.100 feet
Total vertical ascent: 2,400 feet
Trail ending: 11,500 feet
Length: 5 miles (8 kilometers)
Recommended season: July 1 to September 15
Use: Very heavy
Difficulty: Moderate to difficult
USGS maps: East Portal and Nederland
Trail profile:

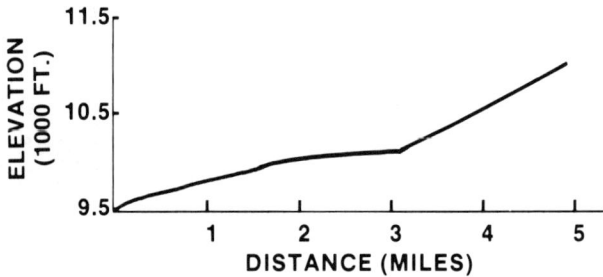

Access:

Access is both from Hessie, which is west of Eldora on county road 130, and by way of a foot trail north of Rollins Pass which drops down into the upper drainage south of King Lake.

The King Lake Trail also provides access to the Bob and Betty lakes, which are about one mile north. In the lower valley, the trail follows an old mining road, which begins on private land. The wilderness boundary is encountered at mile 1.5. About one mile up the road, and a quarter mile to

King Lake Trail begins in this broad subalpine meadow. Courtesy U.S. Forest Service.

the south along a short trail, is Lost Lake, where the remnants of some mines can be seen. Just beyond the side trail to Lost Lake is a juncture in the trail, the left fork ascending toward King Lake and the right fork leading to Woodland Lake and to Devil's Thumb Pass. This juncture is actually where the King Lake Trail starts. Prior to this point, you are on the Devil's Thumb Trail.

Continuing on the left fork, you will enter the upper valley of the South Fork of Middle Boulder Creek, a popular snow-touring area in the winter. To the north is Woodland Mountain (11,400 feet) and to the south are

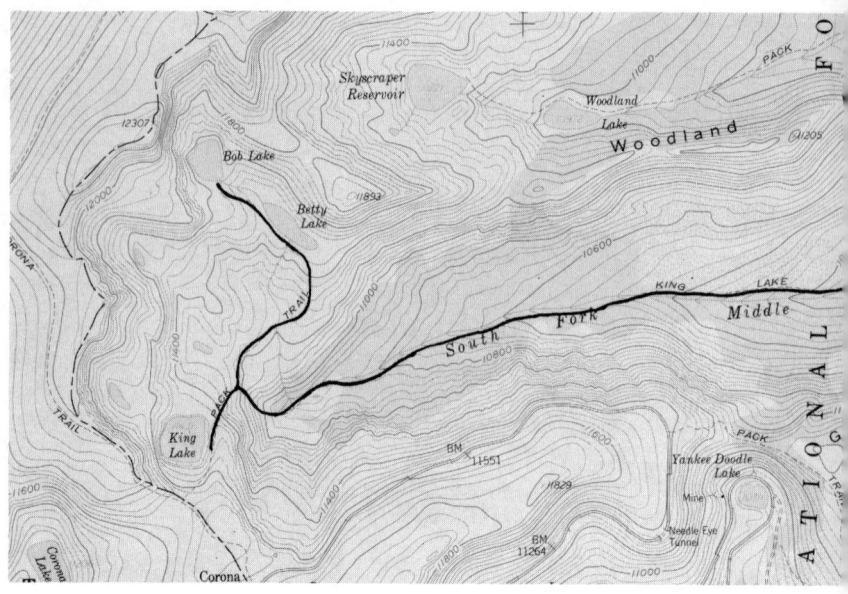

Guinn Mountain (10,796 feet) and Bryan Mountain (11,400 feet). Horses are permitted in this area and are sometimes encountered on the trail.

After 3.5 miles, the trail climbs steeply above the last trees and splits, the right fork going north about one mile to Bob (11,600 feet) and Betty (11,460 feet) lakes, and the left fork leading to King Lake, which is nestled some 300 vertical feet down from Rollins Pass. Fishing is good in all of the lakes.

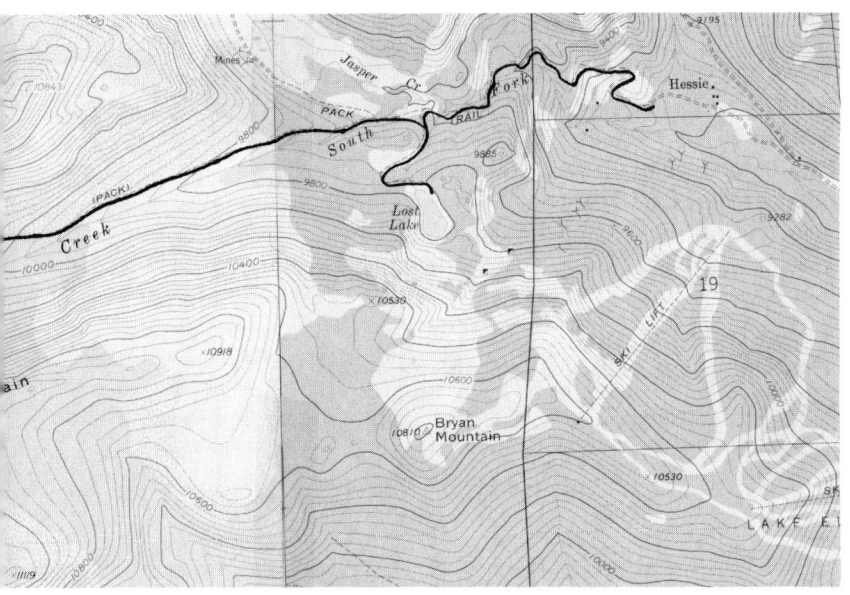

8. DEVIL'S THUMB LAKE TRAIL

Trailhead elevation: 9,100 feet
Total vertical ascent: 2,000 feet
Trail ending: 11,100 feet
Length: 5.5 miles (8.8 kilometers)
Recommended season: July 1 to September 15
Use: Very heavy
Difficulty: Moderate
USGS maps: East Portal and Nederland
Trail profile:

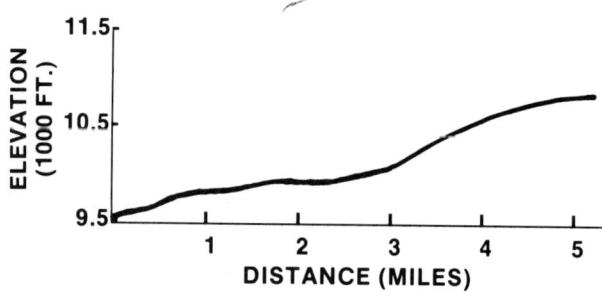

Access:

Same as for King Lake Trail. Take right fork at juncture just beyond side trail to Lost Lake.

As with the King Lake Trail, this trail leads to several very fine fishing lakes with the added advantage of ascending Devil's Thumb Pass, which affords some excellent views both west and east. The country has many deer and elk and offers the opportunity to view wildlife not found in much of the area west of Eldora. Elk are often heard bugling in the woods below Woodland Lake in the

Snow lingers long in this glacial cirque southwest of the Devil's Thumb Pass Trail. Courtesy U.S. Forest Service.

early fall, and bear are sometimes seen foraging for berries. It is hard to believe that less than 100 years ago, this area was the scene of frenetic mining activity, but then, that is typical of the "boom-bust" cycle of mining that has always plagued the West.

Taking the right fork (which brings to mind, in the fall when the aspens are golden, that line from Frost: "Two roads diverged in a yellow wood,"), the old road follows Jasper Creek. At mine 2.5, the trail to Woodland Lake branches off to the left, crossing the creek. Some old decaying cabins can be seen among the raspberry patches on the trail to Woodland Lake. Another .5 mile further

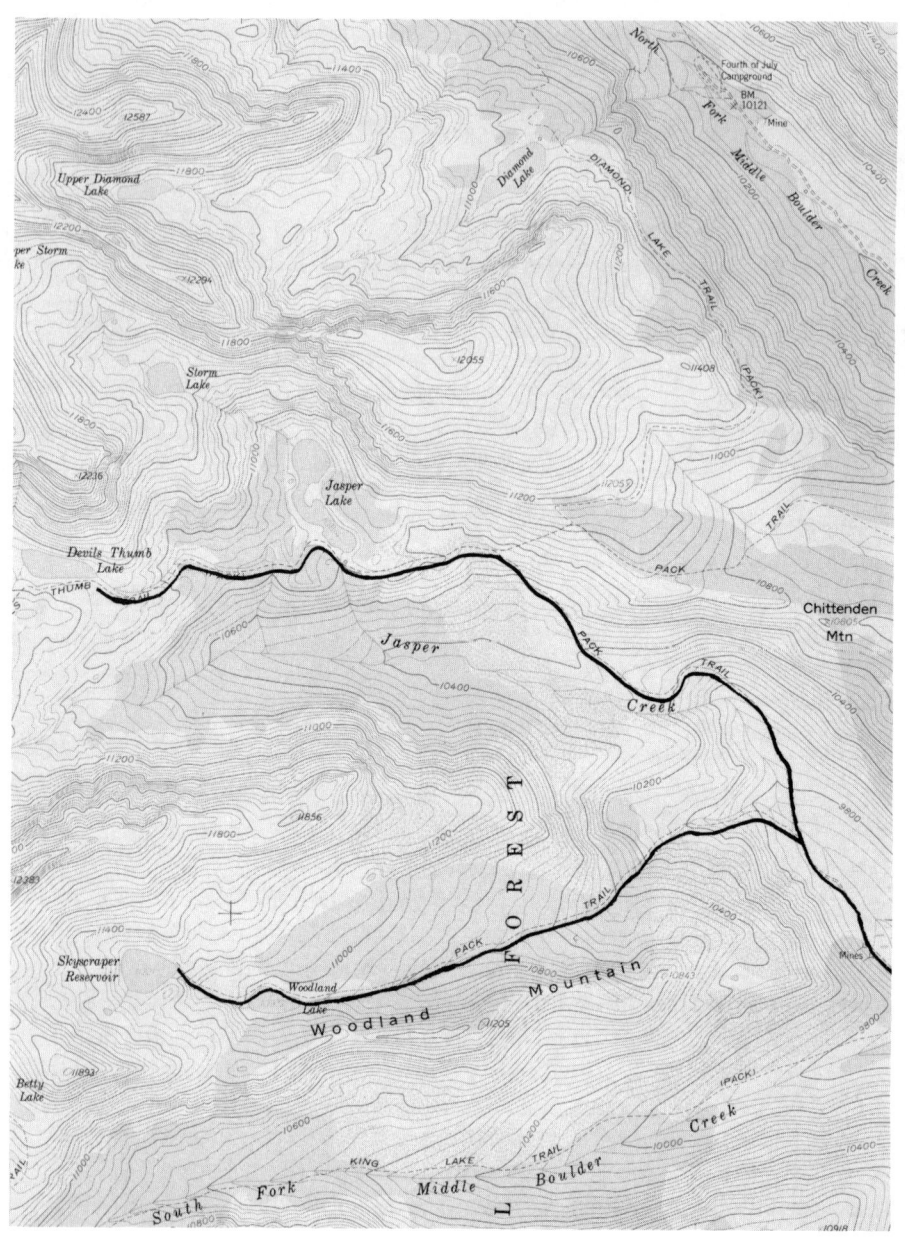

brings you to Skyscraper Reservoir (11,221 feet), located between two ridges extending from the Continental Divide. By ascending the lower ridge, you can then descend to the vicinity of Bob and Betty lakes and return to Hessie via the King Lake Trail.

Proceeding along the Devil's Thumb Lake Trail, you will pass the Diamond Lake cutoff another .5 mile up the valley. Jasper Lake, just to the north of the trail at 10,814 feet, is reached shortly afterward. The trail wanders westerly to Devil's Thumb Lake (11,140 feet), which is only a short distance off. The lake is dominated by the rocky spire which rises in sinister fashion above the talus and scree. The trail continues thorugh some steep switchbacks toward Devil's Thumb Pass (12,100 feet), from which connections can be made with the Corona Trail, which eventually intersects Rollins Pass some six miles to the south. From any point in this area above timberline, deer are plentiful in the summer. Elk seem to prefer the more remote country on the other side of the divide. Those contemplating wildlife photography should always bring a telephoto lens, as deer rarely permit people to get within 200 feet of them.

Note to Devil's Thumb Lake Trail: There is an alternate route on the north side of the creek. This route follows a real trail rather than just the old four-wheel-drive road. Hikers on this route miss the Lost Lake and King Lake trail junctions, but this route is considered by some to be the true "Devil's Thumb Trail.'

9. ST. VRAIN MOUNTAIN TRAIL

Trailhead elevation: 9.583 feet
Total vertical ascent: 1,817 feet
  (11,400 feet reached south of Meadow Mountain)
Trail ending: 8,800 feet (near Allenspark)
Length: 6.5 miles (10.4 kilometers)
Recommended season: July 1 to September 15
Use: Moderate
Difficulty: Moderate
USGS maps: Allenspark
Trail profile:

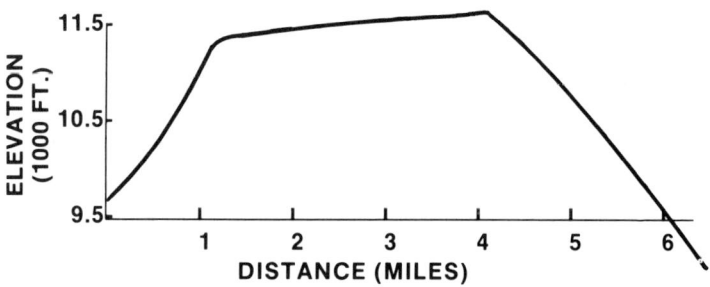

Access:

There are two means of access to this trail, one from the east, near Allenspark, and other from the west, with the approach from Peaceful Valley. The *eastern* trailhead is reached by driving on the main road through Allenspark. Take the first unpaved road to the right at the base of Route 7 (also known as Ski Road 107E), which twists uphill and then heads in a southerly direction. 2.2 miles from the paved road, the Ski Road forks, the right-hand fork ascending the hill about 200 yards to the general vicinity of the trailhead. The trail can be found among the pines on the south or left-hand side of the road. The left-hand fork, by the way, continues in a southwesterly direction beside Rock Creek to a point about .5 mile east of the wilderness boundary, where an alternative trail may be taken to the St. Vrain Mountain Trail. [This trail is unsigned and largely nonexistent; it is not recommended for recreational use.] It is a four-wheel-drive road, however. The *western* trailhead is reached by taking a left from State Highway 72 onto county road 114 at Peaceful Valley, which is approximately nine miles north of Ward. Beyond Camp Dick, about .5 mile down the road, the road deteriorates rapidly. Even tracked vehicles would have problems with it during the snowy or muddy season. It is there that most hikers begin to walk. It is four miles to the wilderness boundary, the road paralleling Middle St. Vrain Creek for the entire distance.

As can be discerned from the discussion of access, it is rather difficult to get to the trailheads in the extreme northeast corner of the Indian Peaks. This can work to the advantage of the backcountry traveler, though, in that it obviously thins out the crowd along the way. People ordinarily take the path of least resistance, which is why the areas to the south are so crowded. This area also backs up against the national park, where, of course, backcountry travel is strictly regulated and held to a minimum. If you can get to the trailheads, there is the rare opportunity, on the Eastern Slope, for a good wilderness experience, even in the summer (though still not as good as on the Western Slope).

The St. Vrain Mountain Trail ascends steeply from the Middle St. Vrain drainage, covering some 1,400 feet vertically in less than one mile. After the initial shocking ascent, however, the trail levels off and follows the contours through the dense subalpine forest, crossing one small stream draining from St. Vrain Mountain (12,162 feet). The shade of the forest is a relief, as the initial ascent

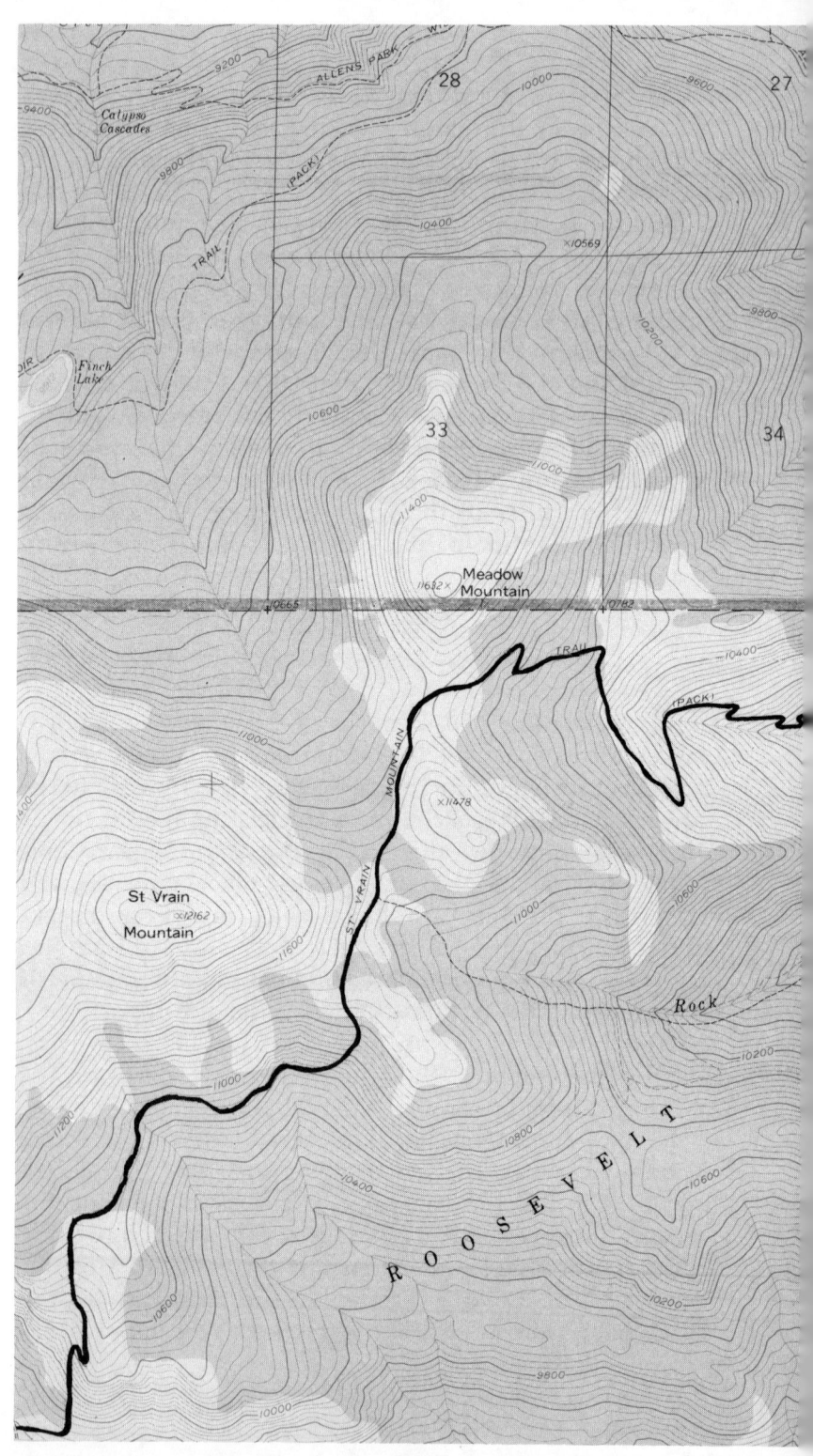

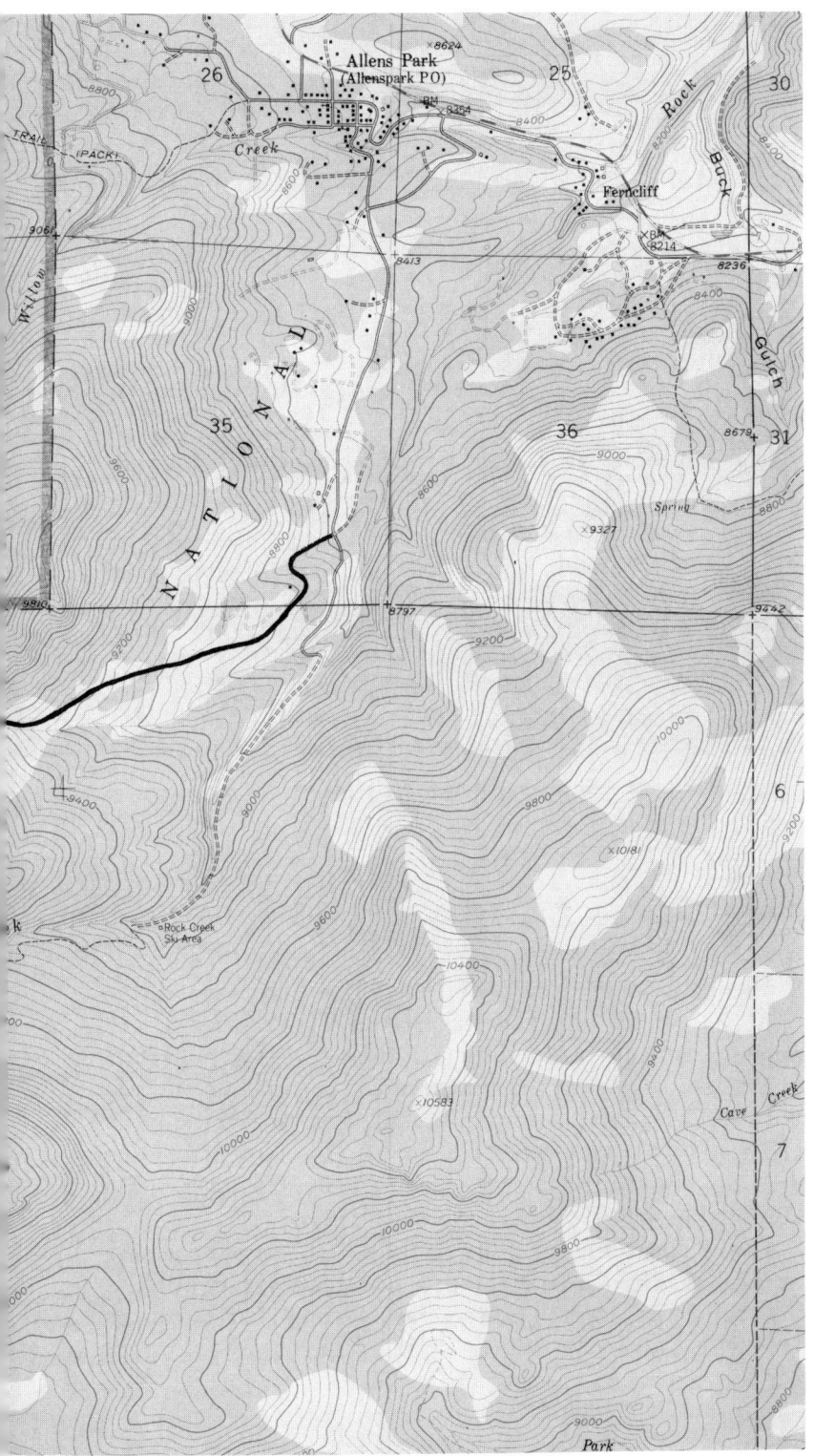

The view from Meadow Mountain (11,632 feet) is expansive on a clear summer day. Courtesy U.S. Forest Service.

is also made over terrain that has little if any vegetation.

At 2.6 miles, the side trail from Upper Rock Creek appears from the right. The trail then enters a small band of timber as it heads upcountry to the bare saddle midway between Meadow Mountain (11,632 feet) and the slightly elevated point (11,478 feet) due south. Deer are often seen grazing, both in the country south of St. Vrain Mountain and in the vicinity of Meadow Mountain.

There is actually far more to the simple act of browsing or grazing than meets the eye. Interestingly enough, a profound interaction and feedback system is occurring as the deer graze. Their food preference selectively influences the genetic makeup of the local plants, which, in turn, determines the quality and variety of food available, which, as a result, comes back to influence the deer population itself. Thus, we see not only the fundamental unity of the natural community in the act of grazing, but also the ongoing process of evolution. This interrelatedness and interdependence of various components of the ecosystem is of particular concern in the high mountains, where life is more tentative and fragile than at lower elevations. A single factor or component altered or removed can change the entire dynamics of a valley or a forest and have complex ramifications.

The trail runs off Meadow Mountain to the east through the krummholz, switchbacking down several thousand feet in elevation. A portion of the slope was recently cleared of timber by forest fire and, because of the lush secondary growth, provides excellent habitat for a large variety of animals. The trail terminates on a spur of the Ski Road.

10. ST. VRAIN GLACIER TRAIL

Trailhead elevation: 9,583 feet
Total vertical ascent: 1,617 feet
Trail ending: 11,200 feet (Lake Gibraltar)
Length: 12.4 miles (22.32 kilometers) roundtrip
Recommended season: July 1 to September 15
Use: Moderate
Difficulty: Difficult
USGS maps: Allenspark and Isolation Peak
Trail profile:

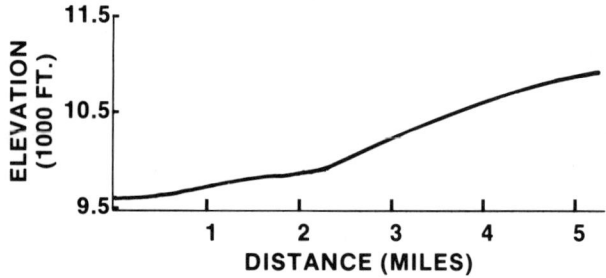

Access:

Same as for St. Vrain Mountain Trail.

This trail offers quite a bit to the hiker: a good climb into the high country along gently sloping terrain, excellent fishing, and a series of spectacular glaciers at the headwaters of Middle St. Vrain Creek. Those without four-wheel-drive vehicles, however, should add another six miles roundtrip to the total distance for the three miles one way that must be walked once the access road turns bad, which is just beyond Camp Dick. Wildlife is plentiful in

Interesting specimens of krumholtz can be found at timberline on the St. Vrain Glacier Trail. Courtesy U.S. Forest Service.

the area, including deer, elk, and bear, and the first two are seen often. Berry picking can be good in the fall in the many blueberry and raspberry patches in the vicinity of the creek.

For the first .5 mile, the trail is fairly steep. After the first turnoff to the left toward Red Deer Lake (10,372 feet), it levels out, still paralleling the Middle St. Vrain as it ascends through a fine subalpine forest. A sidetrip to Red Deer is worth the time—it is a very lovely krummholz-rimmed glacial tarn nestled into the unnamed mountain to the north of Buchanan Pass (12,391 feet). I think that this mountain should be named for the author of this book, but I have not yet been able to find the means to accomplish that.

After another .5 mile, the trail passes through the site of an old sawmill, which brings to mind Hemingway's famous

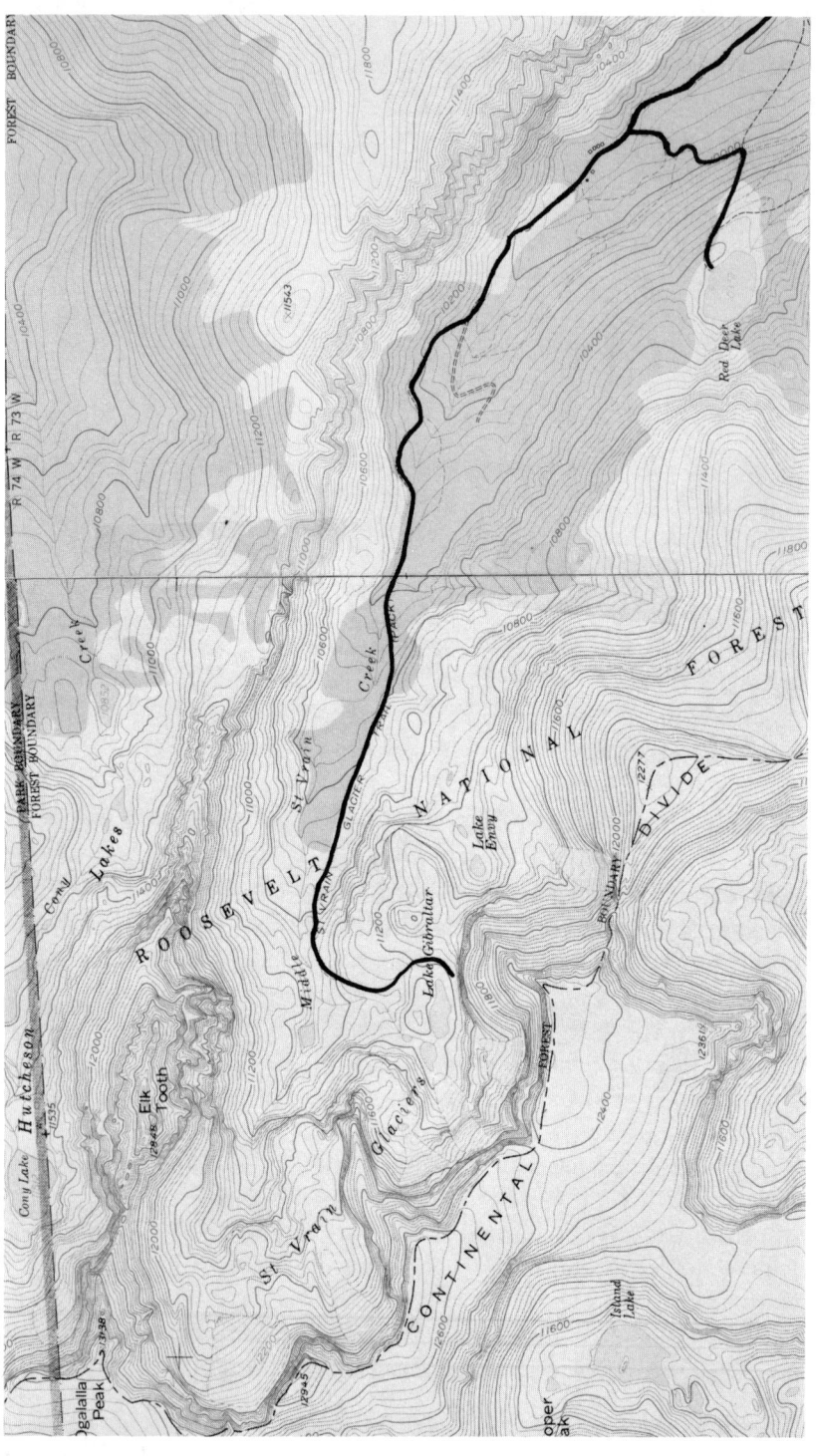

description of the sawmill at the beginning of *For Whom the Bell Tolls*. The setting was somewhat similar. There is another trail back toward Red Deer Lake (and Buchanan Pass) at the sawmill. Following what has to at this point been more or less an abandoned road, you find it now turning more and more into a real wilderness trail. The steep valley walls on either side have few trees. A fine subalpine forest of spruce and fir thickly covers the valley floor. All during the day a chill breeze comes down the valley from the snow.

Approximately four miles beyond the edge of the wilderness, the trail bends to the left, or south, and ascends the final slope toward Lake Gibraltar (11,200 feet), beyond which are the famous glaciers that are the ultimate source of Middle St. Vrain Creek. Across a low ridge to the east of Lake Gibraltar is Lake Envy (11,020 feet), which, in its diminutive size, is approximately named. Towering above all the major and minor lakes in these glacial cirques are the spectacular cliffs in which forever hang the St. Vrain Glaciers. This is truly one of the more remote and magnificent spots in the entire Indian Peaks Wilderness Area, and a good place to reflect upon the wisdom of those who fought for its wilderness status.

11. CONEY LAKES TRAIL

Trailhead elevation: 9,161 feet (at Beaver Reservoir)
Total vertical ascent: 1,779 feet
Trail ending: 10,940 feet (Upper Coney Lake)
Length: 6 miles (9.6 kilometers) from reservoir
Recommended season: July 1 to September 15
Use: Moderate
Difficulty: Moderate
USGS maps: Ward and Allenspark
Trail profile:

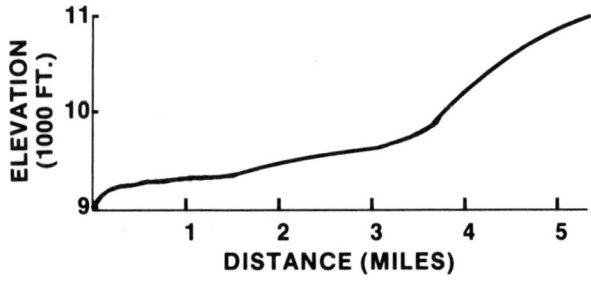

Access:

> Approximately six miles north of Ward on Colorado 72, turn left (west) on the road marked Beaver Reservoir. Drive 2.5 miles on this unpaved road to the trailhead on the north shore. Passenger cars should not attempt to go beyond this point.

The Coney Lakes Trail offers a pleasant diversity to the backcountry traveler, from lodgepole pine forest interspersed with beaver meadowland to aspen groves and classic subalpine evergreen forest to the lovely krummholz

The Coney Lakes Trail begins here, at windswept Coney Flats. Courtesy U.S. Forest Service.

and tundra of Upper (10,940 feet) and Lower (10,600 feet) Coney lakes. Fishing can be good, both in Coney Creek and in the lakes, which are all deep enough to avoid freeze-out and to support a good population of native cutthroat trout. Deer and elk are often seen along the Coney Trail and along the trail up to Buchanan Pass, which branches from the Beaver Lake Trail after a few miles. The ever-narrowing valley up to the lakes is lovely, a classic example of the effects of glaciation. It offers excellent opportunities for photographers to shoot upcountry toward Paiute Peak and Mount Audubon, with the lakes and meadows in the foreground.

For the first three miles to Coney Flats, the trail (or four-wheel-drive road) moves in a westerly direction through a lodgepole pine forest occasionally broken up with beaver meadows. At Coney Flats there is a bridge across the creek.

The fork to the right, or due west just past the creek is part of the Beaver Creek Trail, which joins the Buchanan

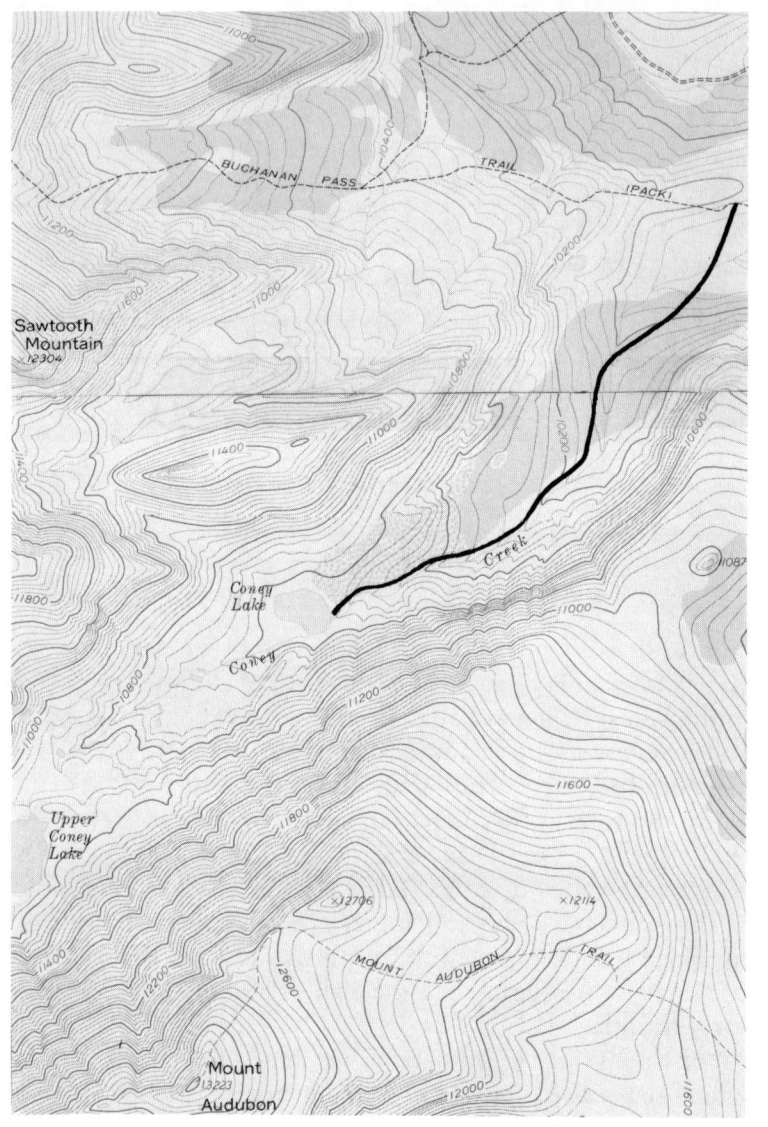

The battered skeleton of a Douglas fir stands lonely sentinel below Coney Lake (10,600 feet). Courtesy Linda Elinoff.

Pass Trail to ascend upcountry to the low saddle just north of Sawtooth Mountain (12,304 feet), and then over into the Buchanan Creek drainage on the other side of the divide. It is three miles from the ford to Buchanan Pass, the trail passing alternately through aspen groves, limber pine stands, subalpine forest, and then over the tundra for the last mile. Sawtooth Mountain has the distinction of being the easternmost point on the Continental Divide.

Following the bridge over Coney Creek, the trail parallels the Coney Creek drainage through some meadowland and subalpine forest two miles to Lower Coney Lake. Beyond the lower lake, the trail becomes progressively less distinct and soon disappears. The upper lake is dramatically nestled in the cirque between Mount Audubon and Paiute Peak. Both lakes are named for the

The Buchanan Pass Trail, pictured here, is reached from the Coney Flats Trail. Courtesy U.S. Forest Service.

coney, a small furry relative of the snowshoe rabbit that inhabits the rock fields above timberline. The coney can often be seen grazing with a bewildered expression at these two-legged intruders into his private world. Also known as the pika, the little rodent has many enemies on the tundra, including hawks, eagles, the weasel, and sometimes the wolverine and pine marten. But his worst enemy is the winter, for which he busily prepares all summer long. The pika or coney is forever scurrying from one hole to the next, his mouth always stuffed with grass and edible leaves.

POPULAR SNOW TRAILS

For eight months out of the year, from late October through early June, most of the Indian Peaks are inaccessible to any but those on skis or snowshoes. In some years, snow falls nearly every day, particularly at higher elevations, during that period. Drifts and snow depths, even in the lowest parts of the wilderness, may exceed ten feet by the first of the year. Consequently, ski touring and snowshoeing are popular recreational activities during the late fall, winter, and early spring.

The character of the Indian Peaks changes completely in the winter, as can be seen here from Brainard Lake in late February. Courtesy Linda Elinoff.

It is important to be alert to changes in the weather, to dress in layers, to be wary of avalanche hazards, and to bring a day pack, even on day trips, with sufficient emergency gear to survive a night in the open. It is also vitally important to notify others of your activities, the planned duration of your trip, and your exact itinerary. If a party is overdue, notify the Boulder County Sheriff (441-3600) or the Gilpin County Sheriff (258-3956).

The great bulk of winter sports activities takes place on the Eastern Slope. Very little if any concentrated skiing or snow touring occurs in the Indian Peaks on the Western Slope, where visitors to the wilderness can have a truly pristine winter experience. Great opportunities exist in the Indian Peaks for a splendid visit during the winter, but the dangers of backcountry travel during these months, particularly of hypothermia, frostbite, and exposure, should not be underestimated. The following are the major snow trails on the Eastern Slope. Most are extremely crowded on weekends and holidays from mid-December through mid-March.

1. LEFTHAND PARK RESERVOIR TRAIL

Trailhead elevation: 10,080 feet
Total vertical ascent: 560 feet
Trail ending: 10,640 feet
Length: 2 miles (3.2 kilometers)
Recommended season: December 25 to April 15
  (varies from year to year)
Use: Moderate to heavy
Difficulty: Moderate to Difficult
USGS maps: Ward
Trail profile:

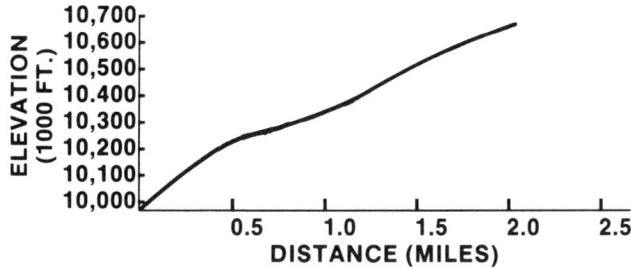

Access:

Follow Colorado 72 north from Nederland to the Brainard Lake Road (county 102) just north of Ward. Take a left onto this road and drive approximately three miles to the cattleguard and public parking area. Sudden storms may drift parts of the road. Chains and/or snow tires are sometimes necessary. Generally the road is well plowed.

The Lefthand Park reservoir ski touring trail is probably the best trail for the beginner or novice skier, ascending

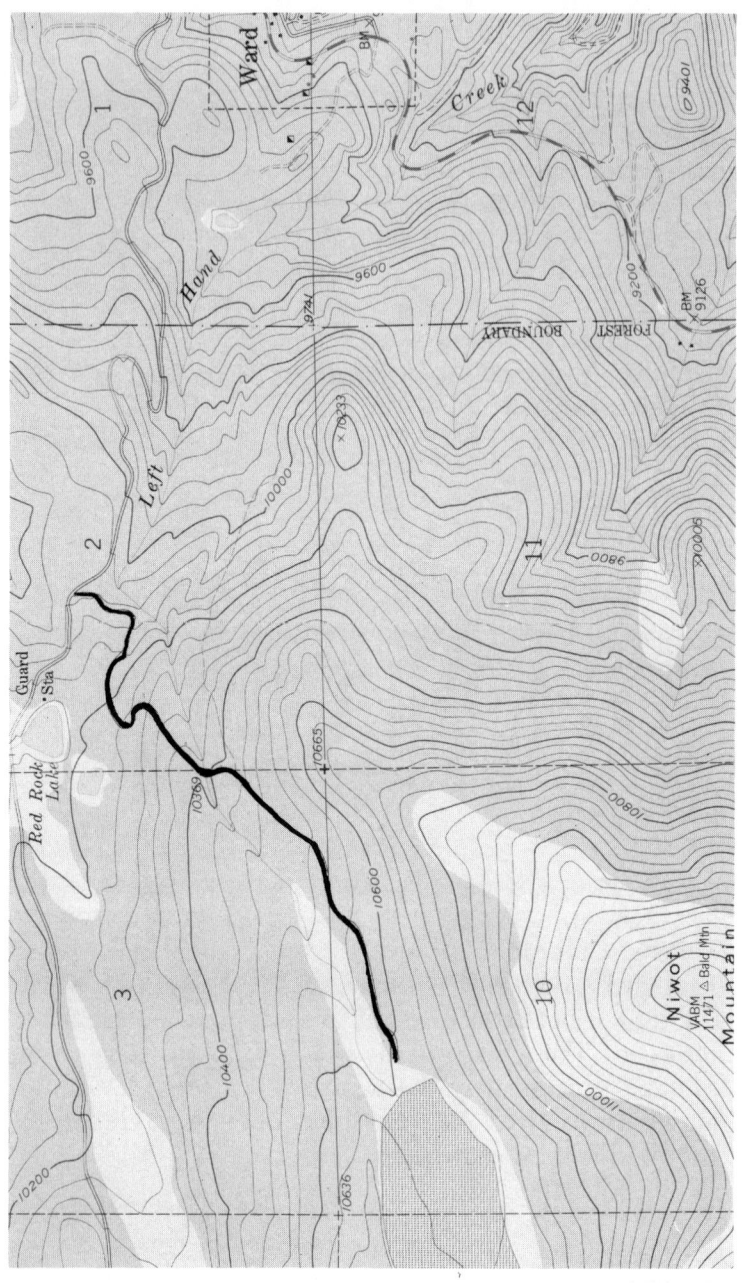

only 560 feet in a linear distance of two miles. The trail follows the snow-covered road from Boulder County 102 to Lefthand Reservoir. In places the road may be windblown and icy. Follow the winding roadbed uphill through the subalpine forest, passing the cutoff to the north (right), which leads to the Waldrop South Loop. After climbing the hill beyond the bridge, take the fork to the right (south).

For the next mile, the roadbed is very nearly level and is an excellent place to learn the fundamental techniques of cross-country skiing, which are really quite simple. Approximately 1.8 miles from the trailhead, a fork to the right (west) leads down into the forest and parallels the creek up to the reservoir. If you choose to continue along the roadbed, the last .2 mile may be windblown and crusted. The entire drainage has some of the highest winds in the Front Range, and a scarf is a necessity in protecting the face from exposure.

2. WALDROP TRAILS
(North and South)

Trailhead elevation: 10,080 feet
Total vertical ascent: 320 (south); 300 feet (north)
Trail ending: 10,400 feet (south); 10,380 feet (north)
Length: 2.7 miles (4.3 kilometers)
Recommended season: December 15 to April 15
  (varies from year to year)
Use: Heavy
Difficulty: South—easy; North—more difficult
USGS maps: Ward
Trail profile:

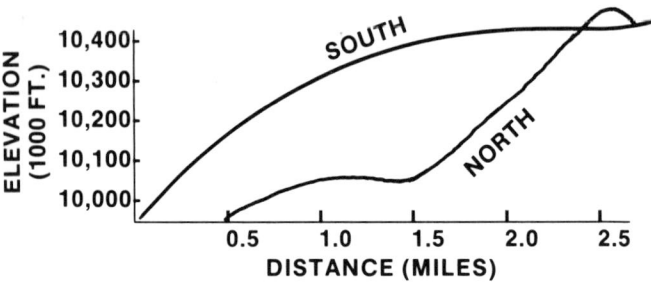

Access:

Same as for Lefthand Park Reservoir.

These trails are slightly more difficult and more scenic than the Lefthand Park Reservoir Trail and have the advantage of getting the skier off the roadbed and into the surrounding forest, which is beautiful in the winter. The beginning skier should probably take the CMC South Loop, whose trailhead is fifty yards west of the cattleguard

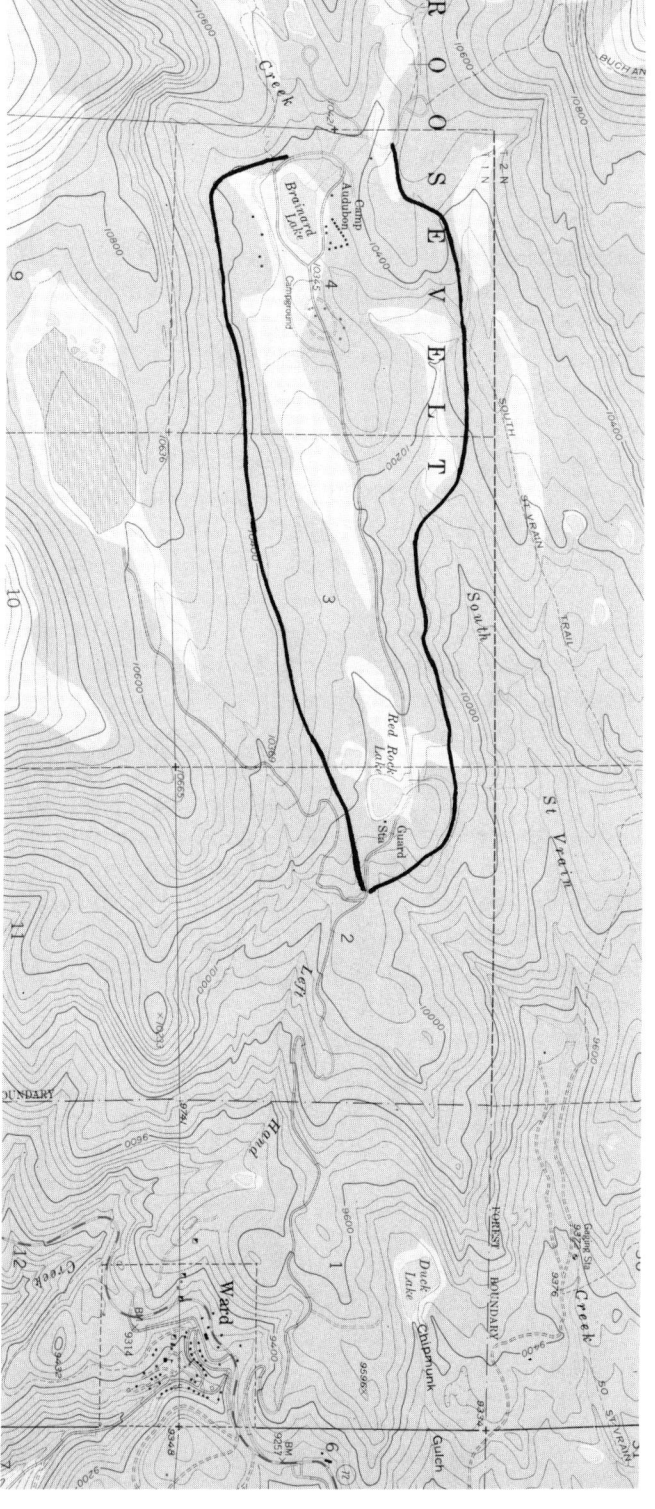

and whose trail is distinctly marked with blue diamond trail blazers all the way. The new "Little Raven Ski Trail" loops south of the trail and is in the "most difficult" category.

After the first .5 mile, where the trail ascends 200 feet, the ascent is very gradual through the subalpine forest and through several meadows between Red Rock Lake and Brainard Lake. Sometimes great horned owls are startled from the thickets of spruce and fir where they sleep during the day, and snowshoe rabbits are often seen in the undergrowth. The trail ends at Brainard Lake, which is a marvelous place to take photographs of the snow-covered crags and have a picnic lunch on the snow. Return by the same route, or, if the snow is deep enough, the Brainard Lake roadbed can be used.

More experienced skiers should probably take the Waldrop North Loop, whose trailhead is found fifty yards west of the cattleguard and off to the right or north side of the roadway. Like the South Loop, it is marked with blue diamond trail blazers and is easy to follow. The first .5 mile is fairly level as the trail progresses through the thick subalpine forest. It then ascends gradually for the next .5 mile, levels off again, and then begins a steep ascent for the remainder of its distance. After about one mile on the trail, a cutoff to the left or south leads toward the Brainard Lake Road. Those desiring a shorter loop trip should take this cutoff, crossing the road to the South Loop Trail. Turn left or east at the trail intersection and return to the parking area. Like the South Loop Trail, the North Loop terminates around Brainard Lake, and skiers have the choice of returning back along the trail, taking the road when conditions permit, or skiing down the South Loop Trail to the parking area.

3. PAWNEE PASS TRAIL

Trailhead elevation: 10,080 feet
Total vertical ascent: 788 feet
Trail ending: 10,868 feet
Length: 4 miles (6.4 kilometers)
Recommended season: December 15 to April 15 (varies from year to year)
Use: Moderate
Difficulty: Difficult
USGS maps: Ward
Trail profile:

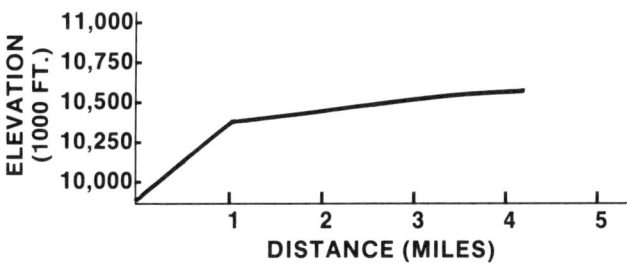

Access:

Same as for Lefthand Park Reservoir.

The Pawnee Pass Trail, which passes by Red Rock Lake, Brainard Lake, and Long Lake, is one of the best touring trails in the wilderness. Generally snow conditions above Brainard Lake are excellent, the crowds thin out, and the scenery is unsurpassed. Heavy winds can be encountered at any point on the trail, and skiers must be in good physical condition and know how to use their equipment. Those

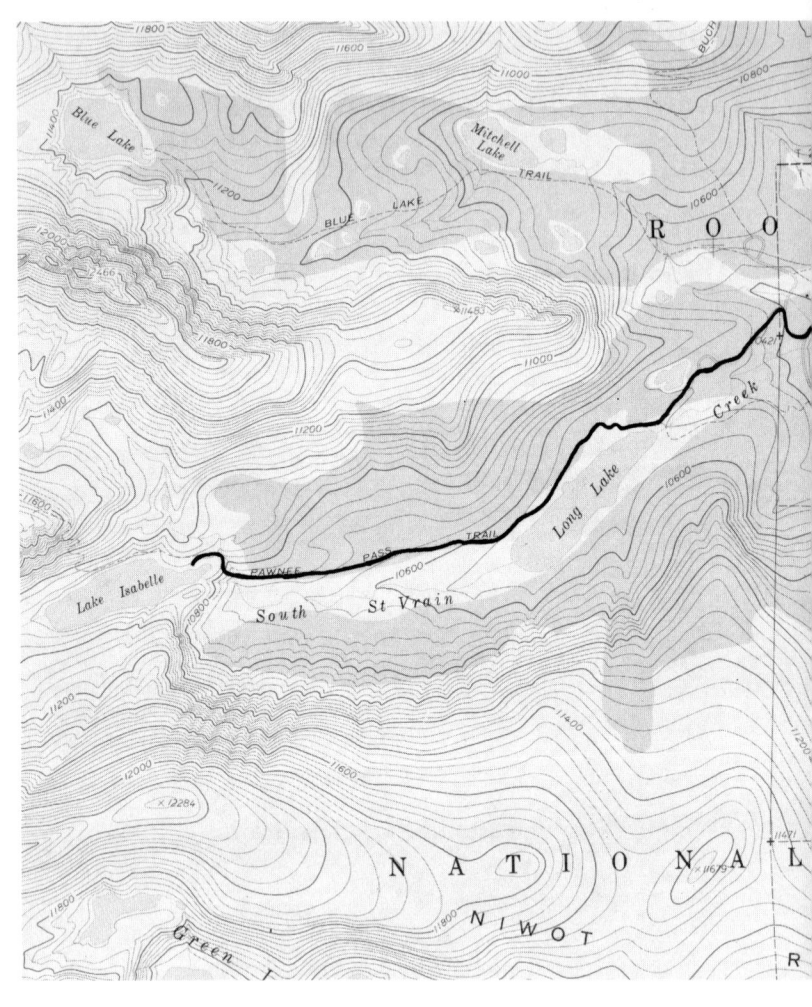

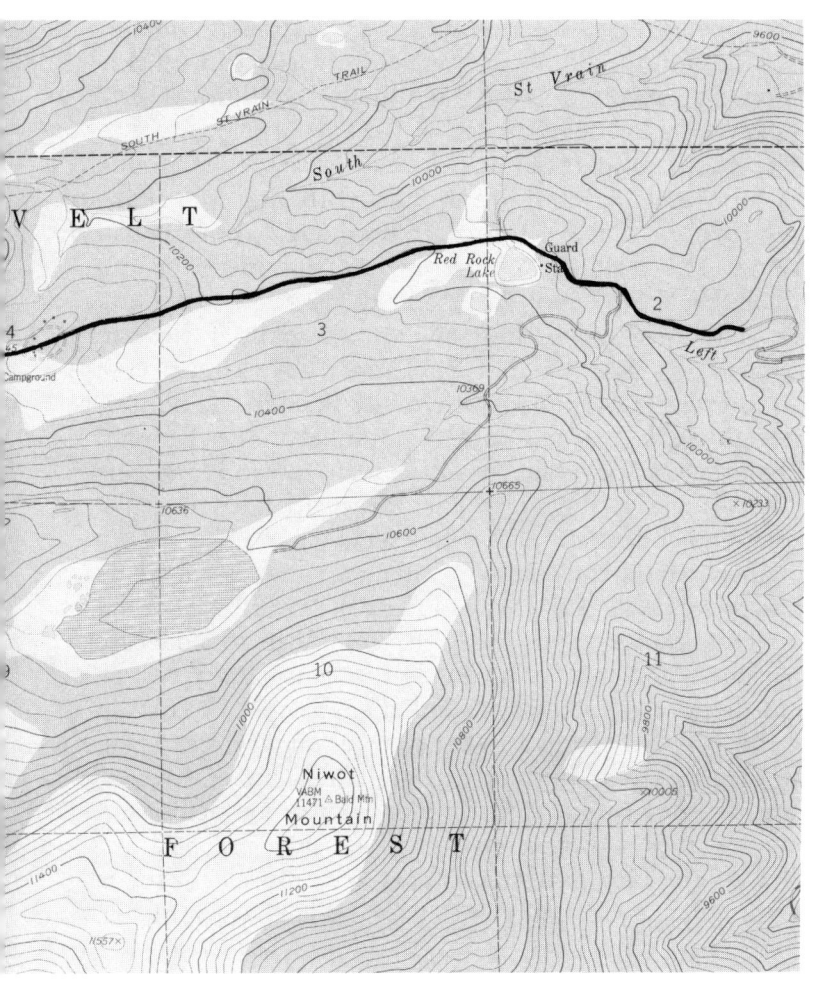

who venture out onto the surface of the lakes should be aware that there is no snow on the ice in places, and sudden winds can blow you over. Be particularly alert to avalanche hazards, especially above Long Lake and in the vicinity of Lake Isabelle. Also, weather can change suddenly in this area, and sunny, almost balmy winter days can quickly become a blizzard with whiteout conditions and temperatures far below zero.

The best route to Brainard Lake is the North Loop Waldrop Trail. At the intersection with the Long Lake Road, turn right or west to reach the Long Lake trailhead parking. The trailhead is just beyond the outhouse and parallels St. Vrain Creek for .2 mile to the east end of Long Lake. The left fork in the trail over the dam is the Jean Luning Trail, popular in the summer as a circuit trail around Long Lake, and is quite easily skied in the winter. The right fork, marked with the standard blue diamond trail markers to the wilderness boundary, ascends one mile further through the subalpine forest to Lake Isabelle. Skiers who choose to follow the creekbed up toward Lake Isabelle can avoid the possible avalanche runs on either side of the rocky knoll at the head of the valley southeast of the lake. This is an arduous skiing trip for those of moderate experience, and many challenges to skiing ability can be found along it. A good way to end a heavy winter excursion like this is to drive down to the natural mineral springs in Idaho Springs, with both private and public hot springs, or to any one of a number of commercial hot tub facilities in Boulder. The hot waters have a very soothing and pleasant effect on the cold extremities and tired muscles. This is very popular in Germany and in Scandinavian countries.

4. BUCHANAN PASS TRAIL VIA BEAVER RESERVOIR

Trailhead elevation: 9,200 feet
Total vertical ascent: 2,637 feet
Trail ending: 11,837 feet
Length: 5.8 miles (from Beaver Reservoir to Buchanan Pass) (9.3 kilometers)
Recommended season: December 15 to April 15 (varies from year to year)
Use: Moderate
Difficulty: Moderate to Difficult
USGS maps: Ward and Allenspark
Trail profile:

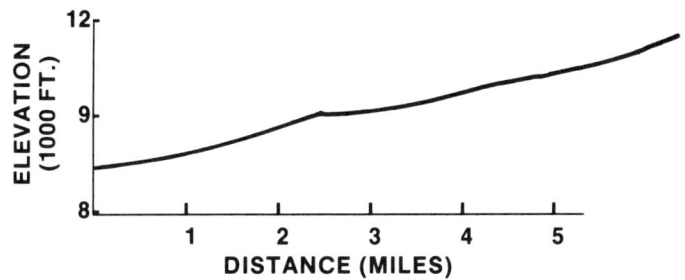

Access:

Drive 2.5 miles north of Ward on Colorado 72 and turn west on the Beaver Reservoir Road. Bear right at the turnoff for Camp Tahosa. Drive west as far as road conditions permit, generally about 1.3 miles. Park as far off the road as is safe. Snow tires or chains are advisable.

For the first several miles to Coney Flats, the trail follows the roadway, where, unfortunately, snowmobilers

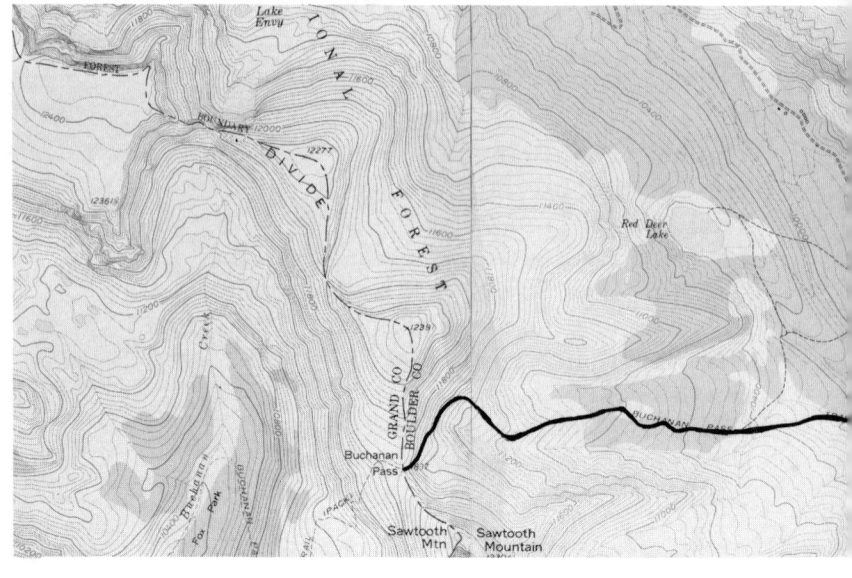

may be encountered. They are prohibited beyond Coney Flats, where the wilderness area begins. Initially the route is very gentle, rolling gradually up toward the flats, but beyond that, travel becomes more difficult, and very real avalanche dangers exist in the vicinity of and in the ascent of Buchanan Pass. Extreme care should be exercised if an ascent is attempted, and only very experienced cross-country skiers should be in the group. The level of exertion required precludes anyone in average physical condition from the trip. Use sound judgment before venturing out on the steep slopes and cornices. If conditions appear at all hazardous, abort the climb and leave it for another day.

Strong winds are normally encountered on Coney Flats, as it is a bench almost completely devoid of trees. From left

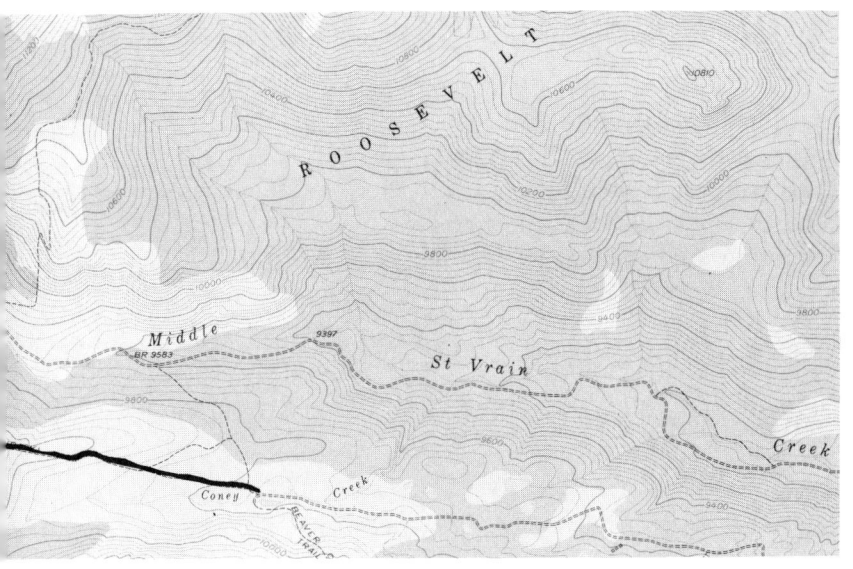

to right, Mount Audubon (13,223 feet), Paiute Peak (13,088 feet), Sawtooth Peak (12,304 feet) and St. Vrain Mountain (12,162 feet) form an impressive array of snow-clad peaks. The trail proceeds in a westerly direction across the marsh and meadowland toward Buchanan Pass, crossing two streams.

At mile 3.8, an area of extreme avalanche danger is encountered on the north ridge of Sawtooth Mountain. The dangers increase as the trail switchbacks up toward Buchanan Pass. Once on the pass, the view both east and west is simply marvelous. It is also windy here most of the time, and shortly after claiming victory, most skiers shoot back down the pass to the shelter of timber and the distant beckoning hot tubs of Boulder.

5. KING LAKE TRAIL

Trailhead elevation: 8,700 feet
Total vertical ascent: 2,180 feet
Trail ending: 10,880 feet
Length: 5.5 miles (8.8 kilometers)
Recommended season: December 15 to April 15
 (varies from year to year)
Use: Moderate to heavy
Difficulty: Very difficult
USGS maps: Nederland and East Portal
Trail profile:

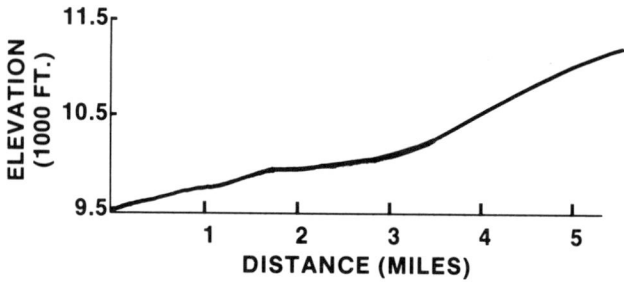

Access:

Turn right (west) on the Eldora (Ski Area) turnoff just south of Nederland on Colorado 72. Drive past the turnoff to the ski area and to the end of the plowed road. As with all the public parking areas, it is best to park with your front end downhill, to make it easier to get out in the event of additional snow.

Relatively flat skiing terrain is found in the lower valley here, with sharp climbs and steep slopes encountered in the

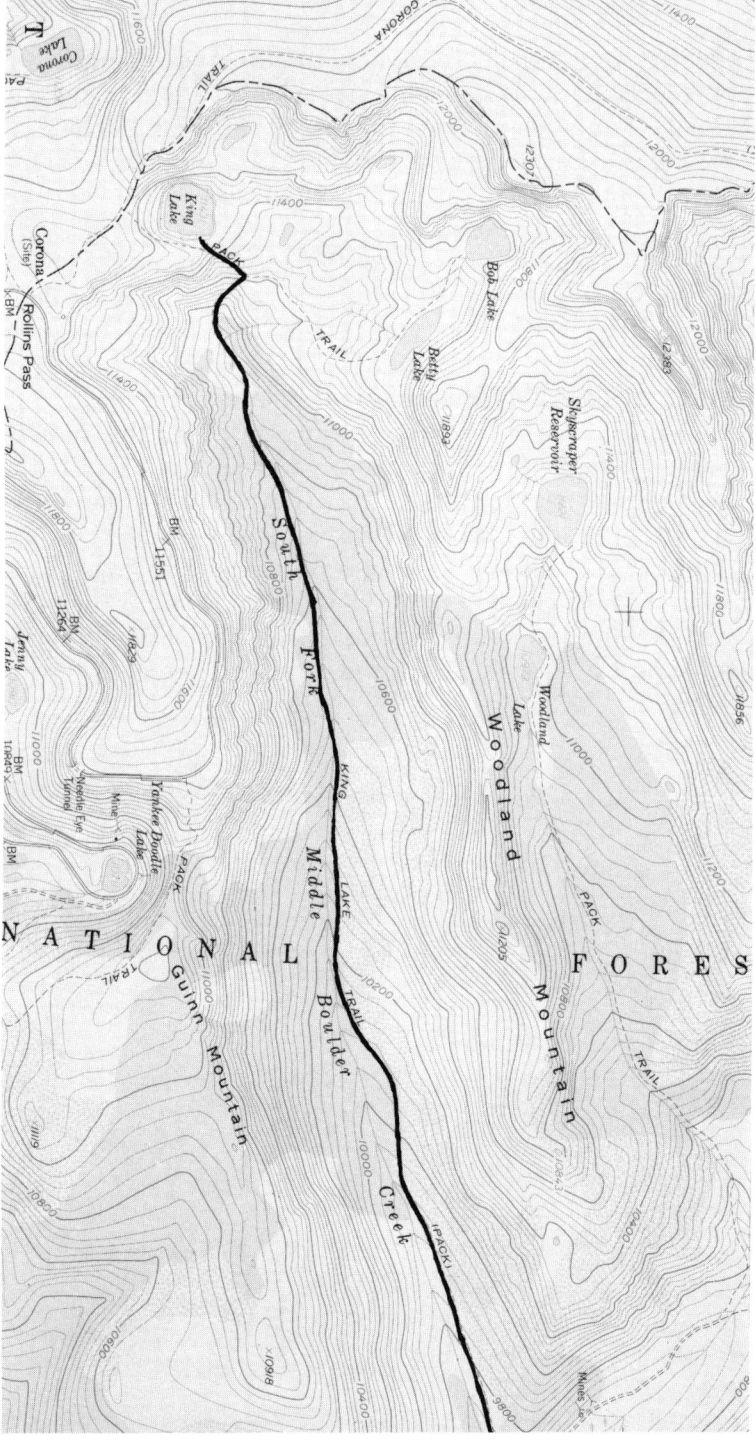

uplands. In the open areas, snow conditions can range from powder to hard pack to wind slab. Skiers should follow the Devil's Thumb Trail from the end of the road for the first 2.3 miles to Lost Lake Cutoff, taking the right fork west for .2 mile to another fork identified by a trail sign, registration box, and bulletin board.

To remain on the King Lake Trail, continue on the left or west fork and ski up the South Fork of Middle Boulder Creek. The trail is very pleasant, alternating between subalpine forest and meadows. To the north is Woodland Mountain (11,400 feet) and to the south are Bryan (10,796 feet) and Guinn (11,400 feet) mountains, with the country around Rollins Pass marking the extreme southern point of the wilderness to the west and south. Skiers should stop about three miles west of the Jasper Creek fork, as the remaining .7 mile up to King Lake is steep and may have serious avalanche potential. The return trip is for the most part downhill and can be accomplished, as with all the ski trails, in far less time than the ascent.

The Pawnee Pass Trail, looking west toward the divide, in late summer. Courtesy Linda Elinoff.

AFTERWORD

All men were made by the same Great Spirit. They are all brothers. The earth is the mother of all people, and all people should have equal rights upon it.

> Joseph, Chief of the Nez Percé, 1877, in communication to United States Army General O.O. Howard.

In a real sense, the Indian Peaks stand as a living symbol, not only to the original wilderness of America, but also to its original inhabitants. Each of its most distinctive peaks is named for one of the tribes that once lived in the western United States: Navajo, Pawnee, Apache, Arapaho, Ogallala, Paiute, Shoshone, Arikaree, and Kiowa. The range, as a whole, of course, receives its appellation from the same source: 'The Indian Peaks.' For so long as these names are spoken, this wilderness will serve as an emblem for an age and a people that have sadly passed from the Earth forever, and for the injustices and crimes, so uncharacteristic of a great nation, that accompanied their demise. With respect to this subject, perhaps the venerated American novelist Herman Melville put it best when he wrote, with reference to a recent battle of his time: "In view of this battle one may ask—What separates the enlightened man from the savage? Is civilization a thing distinct, or is it an advanced stage of barbarism?"

Some places are like some paintings. We return to them again and again. Each time they reveal new things to us: new meanings, new delights. Picasso's 'The Lovers' is like that for me. So are the Indian Peaks. I have probably hiked the Pawnee Pass Trail a half a hundred times in my lifetime (and I hope to hike it at least that many more times before I die). But each time I do I see something new, something different. Like a museum in which many works of art are displayed, the wilderness has many galleries, collections, and exhibit halls, scenes that change constantly, sometimes daily, depending on altitude, exposure, and season. On Buchanan Pass, for example, it may be arctic winter, while, in the lower St. Vrain Valley, at that same moment in time, it may be a hot summer day. But the metaphor becomes irrelevant when mankind, like a felon slashing a Da Vinci oil painting, or like the polluted atmosphere of Rome defiling rare frescoes with acidic condensation, defaces that beauty through malice or ignorance. We must preserve the original creations of nature in this world as we do the original creations of the human mind, with care, thoughtfulness, and, above all, humility. Let us sing their praise, and not compose their panegyrics.

The first true wilderness in which I ever set foot was the Indian Peaks. I suppose for that reason, if for no other, it holds a special place in my heart. Fresh from the Buckeye woodlands and rolling pasturelands of Southern Ohio, the alpine range was like nothing I had ever seen before. I will never forget that first summer. Every weekend my father, myself, and my brother would eagerly set out to explore new valleys, cross new passes, and climb new peaks. "How could anyone," we asked, "ever take this for granted?" And yet some people do. But having come from another part of the country, a place where it rains nearly every day of the year, where the highest elevation is less than 1,000 feet, and where the industrial cities are choked with social decay, filth, and man-made ugliness, I will never make that mistake. Sometime during that summer a freckle-faced, red-haired boy made a decision that the grown man would come to honor: This would be my home. And still, to this day, thirteen years later, rarely does a week go by that I do not pack up my car and head up Boulder Canyon or over Berthoud Pass to visit the Indian Peaks.

There is no sleep as peaceful as that first sleep back in the wilderness after a long absence. It is a sleep like no other, unbounded by walls or ceiling or floor, undisturbed by traffic or noise, unfettered by the appointments and commitments of the next day. You feel your heart beating against the earth, and the cold clear air in your lungs, and you are glad. High above, the tall stars are steady in the pines. A mountain stream murmurs softly in the grass. An owl calls out, or perhaps a coyote. And then the breeze gently stirs, bringing in from the forest, like some kind of potent natural anodyne, the resinous scent of the pines. It is a kind of death, that sleep, that kills all those things you want to see die, from which you are reborn, fresh and remade, in the morning. When you awaken from your first night back in the wilderness, you say to yourself: "Here I am at last, where I wanted to be for so long, where I ought to be. I will lay my burdens down at the trailhead and walk back into that paradise from which I was created and into which my elements will one day be returned. Let the others toil below. Let them worry and fret. For now, for this short time, I will be here. Free to do as I please, and to be as I truly am."

There are as many approaches to the wilderness as there are radii to be drawn from its center or centers to be touched. Some stay in trailers at organized campsites around the edges and just look up at it. Others hike in a few miles, marvel at its vastness, and then return. A few pack in to popular sites, stay a day or two, and then go back to wherever they came from. That is fine. I prefer to hike in deep and fast, and to linger in the outback for as long as I can. Back where there is no one, back where the side streams have no name and there are peaks no man has ever climbed, back before the trails cross the center and start to seek the other side. Everywhere there is life, and everywhere there is evidence of pattern and design, of the mysterious force in the universe that causes matter to organize itself into progressively higher forms of life and intelligence. Sometimes in those places, I glimpse that primordial unity, that natural harmony and procession of which philosophers from Lao-Tzu to Lucretius have written, and sometimes, rarer still, I can even feel, resonating inside me, the same calm, strength, and balance of the mountains I behold. I take this to be the highest possible reward of the wilderness.

In writing this book I had three simple motivations: my deep love and enduring affection for the Indian Peaks, the conspicuous absence of an Indian Peaks field and trail guide in our literature, and the singular natural history and beauty of the region. We live in a fast-paced, disposable culture, a society in which the ephemeral is too often confused with the permanent, the false held up as the true, the easy chosen over the difficult. The means has come to be accepted as the ends of life. The wilderness, above all, reminds us quite plainly of what endures and what does not, of what is important, and what is not. It is not, to be sure, a universal panacea, but, rather, a vital part of the larger round of human life. In America, because of our frontier experience, the wilderness has come to assume a very special and larger meaning. No book, particularly one as small as this, can hope to touch on all aspects of such a diverse subject. All that I can realistically hope to achieve here is to preserve, in these pages, the promise, to the reader, of unsurpassed beauty, peace, and solitude.

Just as the Earth ends on the jagged pinnacles of its highest peaks, thrust defiantly into the impassive heavens, so does language end in its highest flights of poetry. It is fitting and appropriate, therefore, to end this book with a poem by a poet living in Boulder County, a man respected by his peers for the excellence of his craft, a man who often composes his verse in the backcountry of the Indian Peaks. He is not alone in this endeavor. The spectacular beauty of this range has attracted poets, artists, musicians, and photographers for over 100 years, and will still be there to inspire them when this book and its author are long forgotten. Some say that a poet is a person forever trying to rediscover his or her lost innocence. If this is the case, then there is no better place for them, and for the poet in all of us, to begin, than in the Indian Peaks, and places like it throughout the world.

AUGUST EVENING
AT
CRATER LAKE

by Reg Saner

Like a man in the midst of himself,
the map's blue lake going dark
within circles that brighten, widening
from the mouths of trout.
One huge surround of inhabited stone—
and green pine rotting ochre ledges
whose colors dazzle slowly
apart, weave a while in place,
then heal.

On the opposite shore a camper
works up a sweat under fading sky
flashed off an ax-blade. Each downward arc
hits the windfallen trunk as the start
of a silence taking a full
second to break.
No other sound but that . . .
and the flush of high snow, its dark streaks
harvesting cliffs old and roughly angular
as thunder.

A valley that ends
under this dim flitter of wings—
its single bat, then another, drawing twilight
in closer around the lake. And as if
to be taken personally, the first
half dozen stars over water
where even the great crags dream.
How many times will this happen
without me? Here in the simple size
of all we belong to, I sit very still,
the separate steps of a small breath
passing into strange hands.

FURTHER READING

The following books I would recommend to anyone interested in learning more about the Indian Peaks in particular and the West in general:

HISTORY

Devoto, Bernard. **Across the Wide Missouri.** Boston: Houghton Mifflin Co., 1947.
Fremont, John Charles. "Report of the Exploring Expedition to the Rocky Mountains in the Year 1842." Washington, D.C., 1845.
Guthrie, A.B., Jr. **The Big Sky.** Boston: Houghton Mifflin Co., 1947.
Guthrie, A.B., Jr. **The Way West.** Boston: Houghton Mifflin Co., 1949.
Lewis, Meriwhether, Captain, U.S. Army. "Journals of the Expedition to the West." Washington, D.C. 1807.
Russell, Osborne. **Journal of a Trapper.** Lincoln, Nebraska: University of Nebraska Press, 1955.

Another good book, though more about contemporary issues facing the west, is **The Angry West** by Governor Richard Lamm and Michael McCarthy. Boston: Houghton Mifflin Co., 1982.

NATURAL HISTORY

Abbey, Edward. **The Journey Home, Some Words in Defense of the American West.** New York: Dutton, 1977.
Back, Joe. **Horses, Hitches, and Rocky Trails.** Chicago: Sage Books, 1959.

171

Bergon, Frank (editor). **The Wilderness Reader.** New York: Mentor, 1980.

Craighead, John J. **A Field Guide to Rocky Mountain Wildflowers.** Boston: Houghton Mifflin., 1963.

Craighead, Frank C., Jr. **Track of the Grizzly.** San Francisco: Sierra, 1979.

Mariano, Vincent. **In the Ring of the Rise.** New York: Crown, 1976.

Murie, Olaus J. **Field Guide to Animal Tracks.** Boston: Houghton Mifflin Co., 1954.

O'Connor, Jack. **Big Game in North America.** New York: Knopf, 1967.

Udvardy, Miklos. **The Audubon Field Guide to North American Birds (Western Region).** New York: Knopf, 1977.

Zwinger, Ann. **Beyond the Aspen Grove.** New York: Harper and Row, 1970.

Zwinger, Ann. **Land Above the Trees.** New York: Harper and Row, 1972.

PHOTOGRAPHIC CREDITS

Charles W. Murray, Junior is a free-lance photographer who resides in San Francisco, California. He has photographed widely in the west, including Colorado, Utah, Wyoming, New Mexico, and California. Twelve of his photographs are found in the text.

Linda Elinoff is a free-lance photographer who resides in Golden, Colorado. She has photographed in Colorado, Utah, Arizona, Washington, California, Wyoming, Hawaii, and Alaska. Her work has been published in "Outside" magazine and she has had private shows in Golden, Denver, and Houston. Eleven of her photographs were used in the book.

Many thanks also to the Boulder and Granby District Forest Service offices (Bob Allison and Margaret Foster, respectively), for providing additional backcountry pictures.

INDEX

Achonee, Mt., 57, 75
Addresses (Important), 39
Adoneus Buttercup Stand, 26
Allenspark, 132, 142, 159
Apache Peak, 58, 62, 104
Arapahoe Bay Ranger Station, 92
Arapaho Creek, 19, 30, 51, 55, 56, 57, 69, 73
Arapaho Glacier, xv, 117, 119, 122
Arapaho Glacier Trail (also known as Glacier Rim Trail), 116-119
Arapaho Indians, 2, 4
Arapaho Pass, xv, 53, 58, 61, 85, 121
Arapaho Pass Trail (East Slope), 120-124
Arapaho Pass Trail (West Slope), 53-58, 67
Arapaho Peak, South, 5, 58, 123
Arapaho Peak, North, 58, 117, 118
Archaeology, 2-5
Arikaree Peak, 104, 116
Arnika, Yellow, 12
Aspen Tree, 13, 19, 21, 97, 142, 145
Audubon, Mt., 108, 109, 111, 114, 141, 143, 161
Audubon, Mt. Trail (see Mt. Audubon Trail)
August (weather), 31

Autotrophic Component, 24
Avalanche (dangers of), 45, 148

Bats, 10
Backcountry Travel, 28
Badger, 10
Bears, Black, 8, 19, 21, 48, 129, 139
Bears, Grizzly, 6, 9
Beaver, 10, 143
Beaver Creek Trail, 110-112, 114
Beaver Reservoir, 142, 159
Biomass, 30
Birch, 19, 26
Birds, 10, 31
Bistort, American, 57, 87
Blue Lake, 108, 109
Blue Lake, Little, 109
Bluebell, 11, 56
Blueberries, 26, 56, 85, 139
Bluebird, Mountain, 10
Bob and Betty Lakes, 66, 124, 126, 131
Bobcat, 10
Bogs, 25
Boulder Canyon, 34
Boulder Creek, Middle Fork, 119, 121, 125, 164
Boulder Creek, North Fork, 58, 66, 117
Brainard Lake, 21, 98, 107, 113, 147, 149, 154, 155
Bridger, Jim, xii, 3

Bryan, Mt., 126, 164
Buchanan Creek, 7, 19, 30, 51, 73, 85, 145
Buchanan Pass, xv, 16, 87, 139, 141, 143, 145, 159, 161
Buchanan Pass Trail, 84-87, 88, 89, 146
Buchanan Pass Trail (ski), 159-161
Butter and Eggs, 104
Buttercup, 11

Cabin Creek, 66, 67
Cairns, 33
Camas, Death, 11
Cameras (in the high country), 35
Camp Dic, 133, 138
Camp Robber, 10
Camp Tahosa, 159
Caribou, 119
Caribou Lake, 57, 58, 62, 122
Caribou Lake Trail, 51, 52
Caribou Pass Trail, 51, 52, 53, 58, 59-62, 122
Caribou Peak, 119
Carson, Kit, 4
Carter, Jimmy, xv
Cascade Creek, 7, 34, 51, 87, 70
Cascade Creek Trail, 70-75, 77, 80, 84, 88
Cascade Falls, 71, 74
Chair Rock, 57
Cheyenne Indians, 2, 4
Chipmunk, 10
Chittenden Mt. Trail, 121, 123
Clark, William, xiii, 3
Climatology, 17
Climbing (technical), 34
Cochise, xiii

Colorado River, 105
Columbine, Blue, 11, 71, 104
Columbine Lake, 59, 61, 122
Columbine Lake Trail, 51, 52
Coney (or Pika), 10, 146
Coney Flats, 112, 143, 145
Coney Lake, Lower, 143, 145
Coney Lake Trail, 142-146
Coney Lake, Upper, 115, 142, 143
Comanche Indians, 2
Convectional Storms, 17, 113, 119
Cooper Peak, 83, 91
Corona Trail, 51, 52, 63-66, 131
Cotton Grass, 26
Cougar (see Mountain Lion)
Coyotes, 10, 58
Coyote Park, 56
Crater Lake Trail, 76-79
Crawford Lake, 83, 93
Crest-cloud (lenticular (formation), 17
Cushion Plant, 25
Cushion Plant Stand, 26

Daisy, Wild, 11
Devil's Thumb, 65, 66
Devil's Thumb Lake Trail, 128, 131
Devil's Thumb Park, 63, 66, 67, 69
Devil's Thumb Pass, 67, 85, 123, 125, 131
Devil's Thumb Trail, 123, 125
Deer, Mule, 7, 19, 25, 30, 55, 57, 69, 83, 85, 87, 91, 99, 128, 131, 136, 138
Diamond Lake, 121, 123

Diamond Lake, Upper, 123, 131
Diamond Lake Trail, 123, 125
Dominguez, Father, 2
Dorothy, Lake, 62
Drowning (dangers of), 43
Dryas Stand, 26

Eagle, Golden, 10, 146
Ecosystems (in the Indian Peaks), 19-27
Equipment (recommended), 36-37
Eldora, 5, 53, 120, 124, 128, 162
Eldorado Canyon, 34
Elephantella, 83
Elk (or Wapiti), 7, 8, 19, 21, 22, 25, 30, 31, 55, 57, 69, 83, 85, 87, 91, 99, 111, 128, 131, 138
Envy Lake, 141
Escalante, Father, 2

Fauna and Flora, 6-13
Fair Glacier, 75 78
Fellfields, 25
Film (photographic), 35
Fiinch, Rosy, 10
Filters (photographic), 35
Fir, Corkbark, 12
Fir, Douglas, 12, 19, 20, 55, 75, 103, 111, 123, 142
Fireweed, Dwarf, 58
Flatirons, 75
Food (recommended), 37
Fording Streams, 38
Forget-me-not, 12
Four Mile Canyon, 5
Fourth of July Campground, 53, 117, 120

Fourth of July Mine, 122
Fox Park, 85, 87, 89
Fox, Red and Gray, 10
Frogs, 5, 122

Geomorphology, 14-16
Geronimo, xii
Giardia Lamblia, 47
Gibraltar, Lake, 138, 141
Gilia, Scarlet, 12
Glaciers, 15, 106, 143
Glacier Rim Trail (also known as Arapaho Glacier Trail), 116-119
Globeflower, White, 11, 83, 104
Goat, Mt., 6
Goldfinch, 10
Gopher, 10, 27
Gore Range, 91, 95
Gourd Lake, 87
Gourd Lake Trail, 88-91
Grand Canyon, 99
Grand Lake, 70
Grandby Reservoir, 51, 70, 92, 95, 105
Gray Jay (see Camp Robber)
Grouse, Blue and Sharp-tailed, 10
Grizzly Bear (see Bear, Grizzly)
Gray, Captain Robert, 3
Green River Rendezvous, 3
Guinn Mt., 126 164
Gulf Air Mass, 17

Hairgrass, 26
Harebells, Blue, 12
Hawk, Red-tailed, 10, 140
Hazards in the Wilderness, 42
Heart Failure, 47

Heath, 26
Hell Canyon, 7, 73, 80
Hell Canyon Trail, 80-83
Hessie, 120, 123, 124, 131
Heterotrophic Component, 24
Hiamovi Mt., 83
High Lonesome Mine, 67
High Lonesome Trail, 52, 63, 67-69
Horses, xiv, 33, 101, 104
Hot Springs, 158
Hummingbird, Broad-tailed, 10
Hypothermia, 46, 148
Hypoxia, 46

Insect Life, 25
Inversion, Temperature, 17
Invertebrate Life, 25
Iris, Wild, 11
Irving Hale, Mt., 83, 93, 95
Isabelle, Lake, 101, 104, 105, 158, 167
Isabelle Glacier, 106
Island Lake, 89

Jasper Creek, 123, 129, 164
Jasper Lake, 66, 123, 131
Joseph Chief, 167
June (weather in), 29
July (weather in), 30
Junco Lake, 59, 60

King Lake, 66, 124, 125, 126, 131, 164
King Lake Trail, 124-127, 128, 131
King Lake Trail (Ski), 162-164

Kiowa Indians, 2
Knight Ridge Trail, 96-97
Kobresia Meadow Stand, 26
Krummholz, 23, 87, 137, 139, 142

Labrador Tea, 26
Larkspur, Purple, 11, 71, 87, 104
Lefthand Reservoir, 103, 151
Lefthand Park Reservoir Trail (Ski), 149-151, 152, 155
Lens (camera), 35
Lewis, Meriwhether, xii, 3, 28
Lichens, 25, 56
Light Meter, 35
Lightning, 43
Lily, Avalanche, 11
Lily of the Valley, Wild, 11
Lion, Mountain, 9-10
Little Raven Trail (Ski), 154
Liverwort, 104
Lone Eagle Peak, 34, 75, 76, 77, 78, 79
Long Lake (East Slope), 98, 101, 103, 104, 155, 158
Long Lake (West Slope), 80, 81, 93
Long's Peak, 34
Lost (what to do if you are), 48
Lost Lake, 125, 131, 164
Luning, Jean (Nature Trail), 103, 104, 158
Lupine, 71, 83, 87
Lynx, Canadian, xv, 10

Mammals, 7-10
Maps (recommended USGS), 50

177

Marigolds, Marsh, 11, 83, 104
Maroon Bells, 99
Marten Peak, 83, 91
Marten, Pine, 10, 87, 146
Marmot, 10
Mat-Forming Plants, 25
McDonald Cove, 97
Meadow Creek, 60, 61
Meadow Creek Reservoir, 52, 53, 59, 67, 69
Meadow Mt., 136, 137
Mice, 10
Middle St. Vrain Logging Camp, 5
Mill Creek, 69
Mink, 10
Mirror Lake, 77, 79
Mississippi River, 3
Missouri River, 3
Mitchell Creek, 108, 109, 114, 115
Mitchell Lake, 108, 109
Mitchell Lake Trail, 107-109, 110, 113
Moffat Railroad, 4
Monarch Lake, 19, 51, 52, 53, 55, 67, 69, 70, 71, 73, 76, 92, 101
Monkeyflower, 12
Monkshood, 56, 87
Montane Forest, Upper, 19
Moose, Shiras or Yellowstone, xv, 8, 19
Moraines, 15
Mosquitoes, 30
Moss Campion, 12
Mosses, 26, 104
Mountain Men, 3
Mount Audubon Trail, 113-115
Muir, John, 10

Navajo Peak, 58, 62, 104
Nederland, 53, 100, 116, 120, 162
Needle's Eye Tunnel, 5
Nepal, 104
Neva, Mt., 60-62
Niwot Ridge, 15, 42, 103, 104
Nosebleeds, 101

Old Faithful Geyser, 99
Orchid Calypso, 6, 11
Oriole, 16
Orion, 117
Otter, 6
Ouzel, Water, 10, 55
Owl, Great Horned, 10, 111

Pacific Air Mass, 17
Paintbrush, Indian, 11, 57, 71, 87, 105
Paiute Peak, 91, 109, 115, 143, 145, 161
Parry's Clover Stand, 26
Patterned Ground, 15
Pawnee Creek, 75, 76
Pawnee Lake, 75, 76
Pawnee Pass, 16, 84, 85, 104, 105, 110
Pawnee Pass Trail, 100-106
Pawnee Pass Trail (Ski), 155-158
Pawnee Peak, 104, 106
Pawnee Peak, Little, 109
Peaceful Valley, 5, 132
Penstemon, 56
Pete's Cove, 97
Pets, 33
Phlox, 12
Pika (see Coney)
Pike Expedition, 3
Pine, Bristlecone, 12

178

Pine, Limber, 12, 21, 55, 75, 85, 97, 123, 142
Pine Lodgepole, 12, 21, 55, 75, 85, 97, 123, 142
Pine, Ponderosa, 12
Pleiades, 117
Porcupine, 10, 56
Precipitation, Average Annual, 22
Ptarmigan, 10, 25
Puma (see Mountain Lion)
Purple Fringe, 83

Rabbits, 10, 146
Racoons, 10
Rainbow Lakes, 98, 117, 119, 122
Rainbow Lakes Campground, 116
Raspberries, 19, 56, 129, 139
Rattlesnakes, 6
Ravens, 10
Red Deer Lake, 139, 141
Red Rock Lake, 98, 154, 155
Roaring Fork Campground, 96
Roaring Fork Canyon, 7
Roaring Fork Creek, 93, 96
Roaring Fork Trail, 80, 92-95
Rock Climbing, 34, 44
Rock Creek, 133, 136
Rocky Mountain National Park, xiv, 14, 34, 41, 96
Rollins Pass, 5, 14, 63, 65, 66, 85, 124, 126, 131, 164
Rules and Regulations, 41

Sagebrush Meadows, 97
Satanta Peak, 58, 62
Sawmill, 139
Sawtooth Mt., xv, 87, 145, 161

Sedge-grass Wet-Meadow Stand, 26
Sedges, 26
Shelter Rock, 73, 84, 88
Sheep, Bighorn, 8, 25
Shooting Star, 11, 104
Shortcuts, 33
Shoshone Peak, 104, 106
Shrew, 10
Shrub, Acquatic Community, 19, 22
Ski Road, 137
Ski Trails, 147-164
Skinny Dipper, Rosy-Bottomed, 79
Skunk, 10
Skyscraper Reservoir, 131
Snow Trails, 147-164
Snowbank Complex, 26
Snowbed Habitat, 25
Snowdrop, 11
Snowfields, dangers of, 44
Snowlillies, Yellow, 57, 83, 87
Snowpatch Habitat, 25
Soap (use of in the wilderness), 33
Solifluction, 15
South San Juan Wilderness, 9
Sphagnum, 26
Spring Beauty, 11
Spruce, Blue, 12-13, 19
Spruce, Englemann, 20, 55, 75, 111, 123
Squirrels, 10
St. Vrain Brothers, 4
St. Vrain Creek, Middle, 111, 114, 115, 133, 138, 139, 141
St. Vrain Creek, North, 111
St. Vrain Creek, South, 103, 110, 158
St. Vrain Drainage, 15, 16, 75, 99, 103

179

St. Vrain Glacier, 141
St. Vrain Glacier Trail, 138-141
St. Vrain Mt., 136, 161
St. Vrain Mt. Trail, 132-137
Stone Lake, 80, 83, 93, 95
Strawberries, 56
Strawberry Bench, 69
Streamflow (high water), 29
Subalpine Forest, 20
Sunburn, 47
Sunflower, 12
Swallow, Violet-Green, 10
Switzerland Trail, 4

Tabernash, 59
Technical Climbing, 34
Tectonics, Plate, 108
Thunderboldt Peak, 74, 85, 89
Thunderbolt Meadow, 91
Timber, Commercial Use of, 21
Toads, 6
Toll Mt., 91, 108, 109, 111
Trails, East of the Divide, 98-146
Trails, West of the Divide, 51-97
Trails, Ski or Snow, 147-164
Transciever (avalanche beacon), 45
Trappers, 3
Trees, 12
Triangle Lake, 77
Troute, Brook, 10, 11, 55
Trout, Brown, 11
Trout, Cutthroat or Native, 10, 11
Trout, Emerald Lake xv, 11
Trout, Fishing, 32, 83, 91, 103, 105, 143

Twin Pines Point, 97

University of Colorado Mountain Research Station, 116
Upper Hell Canyon Region, 92
Upper Lake (West Slope), 83
Ute Indians, 2, 4

Vasquez Range, 95
Violet, 12
Violet, Yellow and Dogtooth, 11
Vireo, 10
Voles, 10

Waldrop Trails (Ski), 152-154
Wapiti (see Elk)
Warblers, 10
Ward, 5, 100, 107, 133, 142, 149, 159
Watanga Lake, 92, 95
Wastes, Bodily, 33
Water Purification, 47, 114
Weasels, 10, 25, 146
Weather (see Climatology), 28, 32
Weminuche Wilderness, xv
Wheeler Basin, 7, 57
Wilderness Ethic, 33
Wilderness Trails, 50-164
Wildflowers, 11, 30, 31, 33, 71
Willow, 19, 26, 85
Willow Creek Pass, 8
Willow-sedge hummock stand, 26
Winds, Prevailing, 18, 23
Winter (season), 32

Wirth, Tim (U.S. Senator), viii, x, xiii, 103
Wolf, Timber, 6
Woodland Lake, 125, 129
Woodland Mt., 164
Woodpeckers, Downy and Hairy, 10
Wolverine, xv, 10, 146

Yosemite Valley, 98